Christian Poems And Other Radical Explorations

Christian Poems and Other Radical Explorations

Heart of David International Fellowship

Vernon L. Harper

Published by Heart of David International Fellowship
Published in the United States of American
ISBN- 9798647772398
2nd addition

Cover Design: Vernon L. Harper II

Published by Heart of David
Published in the United States of America
ISBN-978-1475221268
1st addition

Cover Design: Vernon L. Harper II

Dedicated to Dorothy M. Harper (Ma)
You always understood and knew the reasons why.

Heart of David International Fellowship

Visit us at:
thebibleinculture.com

Contents

Preface to The Second Edition

I am grateful for you who are reading this 2nd edition of *Christian Poems and Other Radical Explorations.* The second edition is identical to the first, save for the shedding of my pen name "Poet Ntwadumela," the moving of the poem "Parable" in its chronological order and the addition of the Lyric Essay "A Christian Reply to the Reasonable Atheist."

Using my given name in this addition is part of my consolidation and production of my various ministry pursuits under one umbrella. It is my goal to make them easier to find and promote.

I have included the essay in the second addition for its conciliatory tone. Having taken a more satirical tone in several poems I wanted to ensure the reader that my tongue was planted firmly within my cheek when I addressed my atheist readers.

I also wanted to convey my true empathy and respect for those who honestly and thoughtfully arrive at the conclusions of atheism. This essay is an honest attempt to supply the atheist with, at the very least, a new perspective on the Christian faith if not necessarily new conclusions.

I have been pleasantly surprised with the variety of groups that are reading this book of poetry collectively. A nursing home, a drug and alcohol recovery group and a group of pastors are some of the places these poems have found themselves shared. This type of ministry is the reason why I created this collection and I hope this trend continues with the second addition, even to my atheist friends.

God bless you and thank you again for considering this work.

Introduction

This book of poetry is simply a humble attempt to answer God's call as stated in "Parable", at piece in this work. Poetry is important to any society and the poet has an important responsibility. The poet must show us ourselves and the world around us without compromise, failing this he or she ceases to be a poet and becomes something less than true.

The poet must encourage, accuse, reveal, and represent the society around him or her without regard to how that society might receive the given views and observations. Any society that does not value objective observation about itself is a society in danger of becoming the worst that it can be. Few others can stand within a society but speak to it as an outsider as the poet can and must.

The Christian poet's responsibility is greater still for he or she must stay true to the spirit of God beyond their own passions, opinions, and expectations. The Christian poet must speak a message to all people that at times is as difficult to speak as it is to hear. Therefore, God's poet must be an intercessor, representing God to people and even people to God to bring reconciliation and healing.

One need only look at the psalms of David to understand the scope of the human plea spoken by such a poet. One can also look at the prophet Jeremiah to see how the poet can speak for God to a society in need of change. By using these two examples I am not saying that all poets are prophets, but it is not a stretch to presume that all prophets are poets.

This shouldn't be a surprise to us for we are told in Ephesians 2:10 that God himself is the master poet. The word rendered workmanship in English in that scripture is in the original Greek poiema. Poiema is where we get our English word poem. We are God's crafted expression. We are God's poem.

It is in this spirit that I submit these few poems to be a help and ministry to those who find them useful. It is my hope that you would read through these various pages and be blessed.

Vernon L. Harper 2012

And David said, "What have I done now?
Is there not a cause?" 1Sam17:29 NKJV

Christian Poems

Autumn Tears (Gal 3:13)

Tree weeps blood red leaves.
Recalling perhaps tree cursed
sin hung blood drop red.

Labels and Questions

Christian has come to mean
something other than "Little Christ."

Some things like "judge, jury, executioner."
or "Very nice and very fake."

We are perceived as the culture
and its master intends.

Do we work hard enough to
topple this stacked deck?

Or do we plant it, water it,
contribute to its growth?

Christians must live in this world submerged,
this world baptized in Noah's flood.

The questions: "Keep on your helmet?"
or "Tragically inhale the water?"

In any case there is God up above in the light
lovingly working the pumps.

The Double Life Chant

The double life
Is the wicked life
Plus the cover life
This is the double life
The cover life
Hides the wicked life
And the wicked life
Grows on.

The wicked life
Halts the Godly life
And the Godly life
Holds the future life
And the future life
Guards the soul life
From decaying in
The world.

The cankerworm
And the palmerworm
Assault the soul life
Through the wicked life
And the cover life
Hides the wicked life
But decaying worms
Can't hide.

They show themselves
By feeding off
The soul life
And the cover life
The wicked life
Bred the worms and
The soul life

Decays.

The wicked life
Assaults the cover life
And the cover life
Becomes inadequate
For the wicked life
Seeks to show itself
As the cover life
Decays.

The wicked life
Assaults all life
That it contacts
For it is not life
The wicked life
Is disguised as life
The wicked life
Is death.

Turn away
From the double life
For the double life
Always ends in death
All in decay
Can be restored
Be not a fool
Choose life.

The Passion Stated as Jazz

(A title some people will have to understand.)

"It is a terrible thing to be happy!
How pleased we are with it!
How sufficient we think it!
How, being in possession of the false
aim of life, happiness, we forget the true aim,
duty!" - Victor Hugo, Le Misérables

The act of pain is received and self
gifted through the anguished response to love

to and through the father.

This love bleeds through the descending veil of
administered forty-nine stripes. Our only hope

our only chance for salvation is gifted us and

we perhaps mistake it for a ticket to happy town. He died
to make us happy is the catch phrase

we dare not speak or even consciously

acknowledge less we find ourselves seeing ourselves our
true selves in the mirror of the

Word. Christian means "Little Christ" but where

is our Gethsemane our Calvary our ugly place of the
skull, where we forsake this merry go

round laughter and grinning containing joyless

happiness and money. Yes, we cannot forget the

money. Prosperity equals Holiness and this

Holiness is displayed in how we manicure our

front lawns to protect the property values and
important little sensibilities of the neighbors and

appear the good little Christian to the world.

This Jazz is a Cinderella song,
if the shoe fits put it on…

The act of pain through the anguished response to
love bleeding through the descending veil of

forty-nine stripes.

This is the joy!
This is the duty!
This is the song!

This is and always has been our only freedom.

The Climber

(On observing Mt Everest)

Why does one press to climb?
Enduring raw tortured skin
while lungs gasp needle thin air.
Your bones ache with stress and fatigue.
The pain, the peril
ever deepen,
press the soul.

"Because it's there," notwithstanding,
it is madness to be sure,

especially because you are not the first.

I press my soul to climb.
My skin is shredded, and my
lungs inhale stabbing torment.
These bones cry and bend to breaking.
The pain, the peril
ever deepen,
press the soul.

Calvary is for the climbing,
never madness to be sure,

especially because I am not the first.

The Romans 7:15-29 Blues

(These are the words. Your faith is the music.)

That thing I do, I wish I would not do.
That thing I do, I wish I would not do.
I guess my flesh gives nothing but the blues.

That thing I don't do, I wish I would do.
That thing I don't do, I wish I would do.
I wish that someone could give me good news.

I am no good, I am a messed up wretch.
I am no good, I am a messed up wretch.
This body I carry is full of death.

Who can save me from this body of mine?
Who can save me from this body of mine?
I think I'll call up Jesus on the line.

Said my flesh died with Jesus on his tree.
Said my flesh died with Jesus on his tree.
When I believe that word that's victory!

I am no longer death's unwilling slave.
I am no longer death's unwilling slave.
Thanks be to God Christ has declared me saved.

Since Jesus gave me all of this good news.
Since Jesus gave me all of this good news.
I must rename this poem, it aint the blues.

Angel Eyes

Bubbling laughter, a flashing smile,
and eyes that light up her father. At
four this girl feels like a superhero, her
power, she makes her daddy smile.

*One of her mother's coworkers almost
invited her family to church, but got
cold feet about talking religion on the job.
She also decided that to go to that part
of town would be way out of the way for
a busy Sunday morning.*

Velvet skin, long pig tails and, eyes that
look for her father. At eight this girl is still
a superhero but daddy is no longer around
to be affected by her powers.

*A pastor almost set up and evangelistic
tent in her neighborhood but after a
protracted business meeting with the
deacons decided instead to fulfill his
promise of remodeling the restrooms
in the basement of the church.*

Tomboy legs, singing dimples and, eyes
that gobble up the morning. At twelve her
powers affect substitutes, older boys introduce
themselves, and young men circle closer.

*Two church members saw her walking with
friends from school and scolded her intensely
about the length of her skirt and the tightness
of her blouse. They did not however invite her
to church or consider her mother's ability to*

keep a growing young girl in clothes that fit.

A little girl's voice, a woman's face and, eyes
that recede from tomorrow. At sixteen this girl
has lost all her superpowers, for these men
that come will sometimes laugh, but never do
they smile.

Three hypocrites, doing the damage that
hypocrites do, saw her walking one cool
evening. She took their money like *anybody*
else's, but decided that she would not visit
that church anymore for fear she might
be recognized.

A little girl's face, a woman's voice,
and eyes that are brightened by her father.
At twenty she has discovered late, but it is
never too late, that though her daddy is still
gone, her father never left and when she
seeks his face, she always finds a smile.

Angel eyes sharing her father's smile.

12

My Poetry

I am not
nor am I striving
to be
sufficiently nonspecific or
poetically vague,
toying with the truth
as a kitten with
an expired
mouse.

I am
and I am striving
to be
sufficiently specific and
caustically direct.
Mine is not the kitten
but the lion
doing battle for the truth
as its only means of
sustenance.

I haven't seen anybody vaguely
pulled from a burning building.
I haven't seen anybody nonspecifically
warned that they were walking off a cliff.

I cannot waltz the truth in ballroom fashion.
I must the dance of Jacob,
and I've got the limp to prove it.

Mine is not
the saccharin taste
of the rose-colored glass.

Mine is
the taste of blood
from a ruptured lip
in the fifteenth round.

In the fifteenth round
there is no time
for vagueness.

Two Good Versions

Be not deceived,
God is not mocked:
for whatsoever a man soweth,
that shall he also reap.

For he that soweth
to his flesh
shall of the flesh
reap corruption;
but he that soweth
to the spirit
shall of the spirit reap
life everlasting.

Galatians 6:7-8
KJV (King James Version)

Or

Don't play yourself,
cause God cannot be played,
how you step to God,
is how God will step to you.

If you come wrong
it ain't gone be nice,
but if you come right
God will have your back
forever.

Galatians 6:7-8 KIRV (Keeping It Real Version)

Choice

Our lives are the reflections
Of the choices that we make
And these choices shape our lives.

How and where we are at this point
Of living life is the complete
And sum total of these choices.

Unforeseen circumstance present
Themselves to all but our choices
Will create new circumstance to choose.

Circumstance can be hardship and
Create pain but Godly choices
Will create Godly circumstance.

Choosing a circumstance only
To avoid Godly choices earns
Hardship in future circumstance.

Hardships earned or unearned always
Submit to Godly choices God
Works such circumstance for our good.

Our lives are the reflections
Of the choices that we make
And God's gift of choice gives life.

Hardness of Heart

Matt 19:8

As I caress my memories of us
I am again startled by the murdered
marriage freshly dripping from stained hands.

Far far away in once upon a time
we mingled together, living, existing as one.
Now we mingle our fault
as we end our loving life.

One of us has stopped loving,
living, heeding God's voice,
and before there came these symptoms
there came hardness of heart.

If two will hear God
then
love will overcome.
If one heart remains
hard
there is nothing
to be done.

Love

God is Love.
If God is not present
then Love is not present.
If God is not honored
then Love is not honored.
You cannot express Love through sin
any more than you can express God through sin.

Love is an attribute
not an emotion.
Love flows from the spirit of God
through our spirits
and is expressed by our soul.
To express Love
is to express God.
Love is not emotional feeling.
A mother can feel,
anger, fear, joy, happiness, disappointment and more for her child
and never have her Love change.
Love is something other than feeling.
Love is an attribute
not an emotion.

You can always see if there is Love.
If there is no respect
then there is no Love.
When we substitute Love with emotion
then emotion substitutes respect with fear
and or admiration.
Fear and admiration are based on feelings.
Respect is given with Love.
Fear and admiration, you have to earn
and is felt by the one who makes you earn it.

Respect is given when Love is given
and is separate from any feelings.
Fear and admiration are based on the worthiness of the receiver.
Respect is based on the worthiness of the giver.
If you are respected, then you are held in high esteem through Love.
If you are not respected, then you have to earn fear and or admiration through emotion.
This is how you can see if there is true Love,
if there is no respect then there is no Love,
just emotion.

If we walk in the spirit and not the flesh
then we walk in Love and not emotions.
If we do not walk in God, then we do not walk in Love.
If we say, "I Love you," and do not walk in God then we lie.
If we do not walk in God, we tell the truth when we say
I emotion you.

Brothers and Sisters
Seek the Love of God.

To Her Who Has No Name

(Proverbs: 11:22)

Stately, elegant,
beautiful, smooth
as a ring of Gold,
in polished perfection.

At first glance
one wouldn't see
that
she no longer
knew herself.
She no longer
was herself.

At second glance
we notice
lingered covert glances,
appointments under radar.

It would seem
she has swallowed
the lie
that she is nothing
more than
face body
as
men flatter
with using and
discarding
like generic toilet paper
until again they desire
flesh smear.

What word will
make you see,

what phrase will
make you know
that
the Christ that
loves you real
can return to you
your name?

Until you heed
that Godly word,
that prophetic phrase.

You are moved

as a ring of gold
in a swine's snout
thus.

Self Portrait

Do you know who you are?

I have been a wonderful success.
I have been a horrible failure.
I see myself a blessing too many.
I see that by me not one of them is blessed.
There are many who are able to speak well of me.
There are many who are able to speak ill of me.
I think I understand the condition of my nature.

Do you know who you are?

I look into the mirror.
I study my pain.
The deeper I study the more pain I see.
When I try to look away, none of this can help me.

Who are you looking for?

In the mirror
I hope
One day to see
A very small part
Of a poor reflection
Of the only reflection
That is you.

Peace! You are not who you have been thus far,
Neither are you, who you think you to be,
Nor are you who others hear and or see.
You are all of who I speak that you are.

But I…

Peace.

Faith yes.

Seven Poem

1
Brown leaves fall from old
oak. Air is warm in sun, breeze
whispers jagged ice.

2
Bright eyed newlyweds
laugh, hold hands, and know no thing,
but a forever.

3
Antique old man bends
on aged church pew, face carved in
solemn contentment.

4
Christmas subtracts ma's
peach cobbler. Granddaughter's smile
reflects in pie pans.

5
A teenage knife glints
under red moon. Mother waits
in door, heart praying.

6
Hearing gospel heals
like liquid love. Drowned swine lie
prostrate on cliffs shore.

7
Even warm lives know
jagged whispers. Miracle!
Jesus makes life sweet.

My Mother's Poem

(For Dorothy M. Harper)

Her life breathes beauty
strength to all who perceive her
move in silent victory
overcoming thus
unseen mountains with her love
joy laughter loving children
sharing life's most pure
and affirming legacy
unassuming power her
gift to those willing
worthy to receive perceive
her triumphant love filled life.

The Seven Sonnets of Judas

The Feet of Judas (1)

I must the hiding feet of Judas wash.
Though heart be crushed by loved one's calloused heal
This pain that God as well as I do feel,
Is used to slay my flesh on daily cross.
Be not deceived my Lord will not be mocked.
Though wicked schemes do shape me in his love.
The schemers still will reap from God above,
For sowing to the flesh among his flock.
I must in love the steps of Jesus take
By serving those who kiss me to betray.
This love sincere and full of grace will make
Them choose Christ side or will push them away.
If I refuse to wash the filthy sod,
I lie if I say I am serving God.

Judas Still (2)

Is not this one a Judas still, who lies
With loveless wickedness, who tells our God
He is his own while playing in the sod
Of sin, our Lord afresh to crucify.
Is not this one a Judas still, who yields
His heart to envy, hatred, pride and strife,
Who will not yield his fleshly soul to Christ,
Yet claims a Holy ministry to build?
Among disciples faithful Judas walks
And does not hesitate to now betray,
Betrayal with a lifestyle that will block
Those trying to see Jesus on the way.
If we will not forsake the filthy dross,
We nail the Christ afresh upon the cross.

How the Judas Follows (3)

Forsaking all the Judas follows Christ.
Forsaking all; but not believing truth.
The words and deeds of Jesus are not proof
Enough to purchase pearl of a great price.
His eyes see what is carnal from the start.
His lamps give only darkness to his soul.
As others sacrifice for truth they know,
The alabaster box enrages heart.
His will and words of Jesus must collide.
His inner guile starts leaking to his walk.
It starts with robbing the bag on the side.
It ends with thirty pieces silver talk.
The Judas won't take Jesus at his word.
His self-betrayal is the last thing heard.

Grace for the Judas (4)

We all must love the Judas till the end.
Christ showed this love by giving him the sop.
Christ suffers long with all souls he has bought.
Gives miles of loving mercy to his friends.
The Judas must be given strong rebuke
By seeing the Christ likeness that we live,
A life proclaiming mercy and does give
An open door for him to follow suit.
As water soaks a sponge but flows past stone,
Christ love that fills the heart will not know guile.
Then enters evil to the heart unknown.
Perdition's son has walked his final mile.
The Judas ignores Gods extended grace,
Like Noah's world there is no hiding place.

Judas's Chosen Destiny (5)

The Judas now hangs strangely from a tree,
Though offered life receiving only death,
His eyes glazed open finding still no rest,
God swore in wrath that this is what would be.
Though silent Judas speaks to passersby:
"Be holy, thorns and briers do not bear!
The sacrifice of Jesus love with care!
Do not the Lord afresh to crucify!
God's mighty hands make straight the crooked way,
To fall in such while treading on his grace
Is fearful thing for judgment will repay,
And in his peace, you will not see his face!"
Look deep upon this Judas on his tree,
Take care that there is not of him in thee.

Releasing the Judas (6)

I will not mourn the Judas for his choice.
Such mourning is accusing God of wrong.
Yes, judgment fell but mercy suffered long.
If I am God's I must stand with his voice.
God's voice of judgment speaking only this;
To let him pour his own cup till it filled,
And let him drink the cup of his free will,
The enemy taking his heart in fist.
This Judas end may pain our loving hearts.
We see our former brother's life a waste.
Christ ministry was his to take a part.
This heavens gift despised with faithless taste.
I will not mourn this Judas timely death,
Believing God is good I'll take my rest.

Jesus Unhindered (7)

The Judas gone has left an empty space.
It will be filled by God and not by man.
Men casting lots will not undo God's plan.
The Judas by unlikely choice replaced.
At first Paul will be humbled by God's light.
Then unlike Judas Jesus words obey.
Forsaking his old life his debts are paid.
God's mercy and forgiveness gives new sight.
Who Judas for the thirty pieces sold,
And trodden under foot his heart to rend.
Who Paul counted more valuable than gold.
This Jesus will discern the hearts of men.
Right now your heart is bare before his face.
Are you a one that Jesus must replace?

Islands

Sometimes my brother does not smile at me,
though I extend my hand to his
over and over again,
sometimes he does not smile at me.

When he does not smile at me, I say...
"Let Chloe's house report no contentions among us. There is no need for us to fight denomination against denomination. My brother, let us reason together on one accord."

If he still does not smile at me, I say...
"Pay no attention to the color of my skin my brother, my friend. God does not care if I am darker or perhaps lighter than you. It is of no consequence for we are all members of the same Holy nation and ours is the common blood of Christ."

If he still does not smile at me, I say...
"Do not attempt to look down on me if I am a woman for God has said there is no longer Jew nor Greek, slave nor free, male nor female for Christ is all and in all."

If he still does not smile at me, I say...
"Selfish ambition and petty attitudes have no place in God's plan for this is God's ministry. My brother, my loved one, I will serve you gladly for the greatest of all must be the servant of all therefore turn your anger aside."

If he still does not smile at me, I say...
"Take no heed to those who say that I am poor and not worthy of a place among you. Do not look at my inexpensive clothes and frown. We are both part of the

same royalty and salvation is not a matter of outward appearance."

If he still does not smile at me...
With a tear in my eye and "praise the Lord" on my lips I shake the dust from my feet and trod the heavy path to reluctant isolation.

And then...my brother smiles at me.

Haiku Sketches

"God Bless You!" should have
balm on the tip instead of
sharp points all around.

Today's sacrifice;
not bulls or rams but only
a few hours' sleep.

Jesus knows me still
he sends to me no letter
of resignation.

Pharisee gags his
beliefs down the throat of one
who would taste Jesus.

Sex sin is shard from
early pain, anger, doubt, fear.
Our cracked childhood screams.

Eternity weeps
on a tall blue sunny day.
Souls drop like hung men.

God moves through our life
as trainer, coach, advocate...
Race hard for the prize.

A Tale of Two Sisters

Ann came out to bible study.
Missy stayed at home.
Missy called Ann a "Busy Body"
When Missy got on the phone,

Missy stayed home for Tuesday night prayer,
Ann was there every week.
Ann was real sweet to folk everywhere.
Missy could barely speak.

Ann thanked God for what she had,
But Missy complained for more.
Ann blessed those that had it bad,
But Missy locked up her door.

It was time for blessings to come
And Ann received from her master.
Missy can't make the devil run
And put the blame on her pastor.

Now imagine this if you will
A clear mirror in your right hand,
Who is it that you are seeing,
Sister Missy or sister Ann?

Ma Boo

(For Mother Bentley)

The first time that I saw her there was fire
And love and that mixture moved throughout the
Room blessing all that would receive from Christ.

A college dorm is the last place you would
Expect a mother in Zion to move
Freely, unfettered, fire love flowing.

Mixed with humor and her infectious smile
Was a strong dose of truth, conviction, and
Encouragement. God's love personified.

Years later this ministry was flowing
Undimmed as I sat at her hospital
Bed. "Son, iron wears out. God didn't call you

To everything ministry. Even our
Lord took time to rest. You can work yourself
To death if you want to but these saints will

Replace you and in six months half of them
Won't remember your name. God has worked it
Out that if you take time to rest the church

Around the world will survive for one day."
I am rescued by a nurse who stops in
The doorway. She sees me and hesitates.

"It's ok baby you need me?" The nurse
Answers: "It wasn't that important I
will stop again before my shift is up."

"Sweet girl, just needs Jesus love." She holds my

Eyes in hers. "Just about finished my course.
I have got just a few more days to work,

But you still have work to do, pace yourself.
Now stop that sad face at the truth. We both
Know that this body is just about done.

Son, though this earthly tabernacle be
Dissolved I have a building eternal
In the heavens. I'm ready, let me go.

My savior got me out of the junk pile
And put me in heavenly places with
Him. My life has been good and now heaven!

Now you need to consider that it might
Be important for folk to see how I
Die, they have already seen how I lived."

I see the wisdom in her words, she served
Her Lord, her pastors and church family
touching hundreds and through them thousands.

I rise to leave, and she takes my hand. "Son
When you meet me in heaven, we will have
A time! But don't you rush to get there. Rest!"

I smile and nod through the clouds in my eyes.
"Son, I love you, but Jesus loves you more."
Around me flaming love swirls and strengthens.

My smile broadens despite myself. She gives
Her signature wink and nod and that smile.
"If you see that nurse tell her to come in."

She went home to be with her Lord two days
Later. At her home going the tears where

Mine but the smile was the one she gave me.

In this life she loved freely, smiled often,
Ministered Christ graciously and was loved.

Who Else but God?

I look to thee my God
To keep me on the path
This narrow path I trod
No other help I have

Who else but you can know
This weary pain I feel
You fight my wicked foe
You feed my soul it's meals

There is no other place
My lonely soul can hide
And when I seek your face
You're always by my side

So when my knees grow weak
None else but you I seek

Eutychus

(Acts 20:7-12)

He was in a place,
a lofty place,
full of light and truth
and that warm family feeling.

He, like too many others,
was drawn to the outer edges
of what he failed to see was life,
the only life there is,
the only life there ever will be.

Becoming bored with the life
he perched in the window
to watch the world go by,
and in the watching
was enticed into a sleep,
the sleep of the world,
the sleep of the blind.

First came the sleep,
then came the fall,
the fall from the lofty place,
the fall to the world below.

Praise be to God for the Called of God
who can snatch from blindness,
who can snatch from death,
the ones who fall to the world below.

And Eutychus, sweet Eutychus,
angel touched one thousand times upon
his face and cheek,
though he fell to the world dead

was taken home alive
to live again in the lofty place.

Watch closely the windows
for the world still calls.

We must keep him awake!
We must keep them awake!
Our Eutychus.

Hypocrite

Wickedness glazed with
name and reputation of
God that won't be mocked.

I Am Afraid

Afraid for slaves of the polite world's vice
Who learn what to serve in cold worldly pews
Where taught to fit in like so many screws
Discarding away that pearl of great price.
Afraid for those who try to serve the Lord
By mowing their lawns keeping them so nice
And gifting orphans once a year or twice
But their hearts belong to this fallen world.
Afraid to serve this system's fallen mind
Which shapes this world in anger and in pain,
Who without Christ has rendered all men blind,
And caused their hearts to carry common stain.
We should not be afraid of this world scorn
But living as though Christ has not been born.

The Eyes Have It.

The lamp of the body
is the eyes,
not the lamp of the soul,
not the Lamp of the Spirit,
but the lamp of the body.

If our eyes
(sought after desire,)
is good
then the whole body
(affections, appetites, self-protections,)
will be full of light.

But if our sought-after desire
(our eyes)
lingers on, hesitates over, drinks in
darkness
then our
affections, appetites, self-protections
(body)
will be full of darkness.

Job made a covenant with his eyes,
a deal with his lamp:
"I won't let you linger on sin
and you won't fill my body with darkness."

We say we are what we eat,
but rather we are
(affections, appetites, self-protections,)
what we see.

When the pressure is on
it reveals us.

when we are hurt, frightened, pressed,
where do our eyes
turn?

Where our eyes turn
under pressure
tells us what we really are,
what we really love.

Jesus uses pressure
to turn our eyes
toward him,
and he is the light.

He fills our bodies
with himself,
and in him is no darkness at all.

The lamp of the body
is the eyes.

Keep your lamp full of light,
your body full
of Jesus.

Lyric

It's for them we should be praying,
They are ones who say, "We Hate!"
The most tragic way of saying
That my hurt or fear is great.

Tribulation Earthquake Poem

Silla bowls of wrath (this scrib
And) cause dee saken , of world is
Pray king will cause the fall(Lo) (lower)
And come ing a part , of (B) earth
Surf us writ hing down cit (y) vents
Somemo k ings in world.

Cup fools of wrath stag her and poor.
Ow tt confuse (is)say won t under
Stand under dee p resser long. (Thoughts and)
Real iland(tys) our sunk k an da get d ark
Said No ah but it is go na ll red y
F(l)ew a way for son(m). people is cape
Canaveral raptur . ning WO ver a
Knew lie ff . for eny lef (t)ribula shun
The truth. sh hell fish, people cook th him
Near Wo shun or in lake . afire Wo nttake A
long time. Seconds (de ath) is all.

Judgment Jezebel

(2nd Kings 9:30-37, Rev 2:20-23)

Attached to perceived influence
you quiver and taste blood
like yesterday's leech.

A web of ugliness dances around you.
Within these controls and lying affections
the innocent are consumed at your leisure.

Those who practice the perceived weaknesses
love, goodness, mercy, submission
earn your hard-eyed malice,
your cruelly laughing contempt.

Truth will always destroy you
therefore, you kill the prophets,
preserving your deception,
gateway to your lair.

But Elijah has survived.

Your religion proves false!
Jehu at the window!
The eunuchs cast down their chosen bondage!

You are hillside dog dung, save...
Hands that took hold of folly.
Feet that pursued wickedness.
Scull that carried angry seductions.

Warnings of the judgment Jezebel.

You have been given space.
You have chosen.

You will receive.

The Idea

Son of Man, Jesus
triumphant walk on the sea,
bidding me follow

Through A Glass Darkly

(1 Corinthians 13:12)

Salty tears run swiftly
Like hot wax down a burning candle.
Your problems loom large,
Shadowing your peace of mind.
There is no natural hope to turn to.
But victory is already yours,
And hope has always been yours,
For the spirit has hope
All its own
And this is what we live on.

See Jesus, our sweet Jesus,
Through the tender veil
Of the darkened glass
For this is what we live on.

Monotone hellos and goodbyes move dryly
Like rancid dust over cold concrete.
These people pass you coolly
And sometimes they lash out.
Some people of this world our cold and cruel
And nothing in your flesh wants to love them.
But then you love them anyway
And feel a joy in doing it,
For the spirit has love
All its own
And this is what we live on.

See Jesus our sweet Jesus,
Through the tender veil
Of the darkened glass
For this is what we live on.

Sweet hallelujahs flow freely
Like maple syrup over warm pancakes.
The worship is high and moving higher still,
We bask in joy unspeakable
And praise the name of God.
There is nothing our eyes see
That can make us feel this way,
But we see Jesus sweetly
And sweeter shall we see him,
For the spirit has sight
All its own
And this is what we live on.

See Jesus, our sweet Jesus,
Through the tender veil
Of the darkened glass
For this is what we live on.

Homeless Scream

The heart of God weeps.
Soft snow harsh on cardboard roof.
Torn plastic screams ice.

Grate sleeper in the
shadow of our heart's gravestone.
Our seared conscience screams.

Homeless flower screams
silent lament on tip toe,
"Where is my Christian!?"

I scream you scream we
all scream for ice scream, but now...
homeless scream at us.

The Condition Our Condition Is In

The majority says little, much says the frenzied few.
Hidden little babies killed by hidden little choices,
Hushed from this world but not mute, we are deaf to their voices.
In heaven do you think these babies cheer our right to choose?
Young girl abused grows unhealed and is left without defense.
Chooses lifestyle and is used as a recruiting example.
A young boy chooses same as former victim has ample
Cover to plunder that hurting soul of its innocence.
There must be something someone could be doing for them girl.
Well yea, I'd like to help them, if anyone really can,
But our budget isn't big enough for reaching the world.
There's no time, Friday got to check out this new Christian band.
Our ears become deaf blind and hollow our poisoned dead eyes
When we sacrifice our mission for worldly compromise.

Apology

Marriage is the union of two souls,
bone of bone,
flesh of flesh,
two souls blended in love,
and
God
    Is
        Love.
Without God means without love.
All that remains is fleshly emotion,
soulish feeling.

How can two walk together
unless they agree,
Godly love to Godly love
or
fleshly emotion to fleshly emotion?

When a man finds a wife
he has found a good thing,
she becomes the man's choice,
the man's responsibility.

When seeking to choose a wife
a man must first seek God,
forsaking all fleshly emotion,
learning Godly love from the Father
as he is instructed by the word.

If a man does not seek God,
but chooses from fleshly emotion
then love will be absent from the marriage
in the man and or the wife.

If the marriage, then is shipwrecked
it is the man's responsibility,
for it is the man who chooses wife,
how and why his choice was made
belongs only to the man.

Therefore

the wife must be loved of the man
as the church is loved of Christ,
from Gethsemane to Golgotha
until his flesh is crucified.

Then

the man can say to the father
"Tetelestai" (It is finished),
gifting his wife his sacrifice
to be cherished or rejected
embraced or cast away.

But

whether cherished or rejected
the man is still responsible
for every wrong done in his marriage.

So

I apologize.
I, apologize to you.
I apologize for every hurt, betrayal, deception
I have done
to me
of you.

Daddy

Daddy I can't see you
I see...the fixed bikes, the rescued cat,
that bit through your glove.
I see...the trips to the park
where we all posed on the plastic
pony, like clowns at a circus rodeo.
They are gone
from memory
save the faded
pictures
that we took.
And they are...
fading...
still.

We
don't
talk.
Daddy I can't hear you.
I hear... the rumbling of the truck that took us giggling
and wide eyed
to the airport to watch the planes take off.
I hear the rushing of the wind
from the engines
that blew hot
air into my face,
and sent
Clarence and I laughing
and stumbling
down
the sidewalk trying to
out run
my cap.
I hear... the monkeys in your truck

that were supposed to go straight
from the airport to the zoo
but you stopped
at home
so that we could see them,
and become celebrities with all the other
seven and nine-year old's.
We have grown...
long past...
nine or celebrities
and we are
growing
still.

We
don't
talk.
Daddy I can't feel you.
I feel...the hurt in your voice
when you proclaim,
"I'm an army man,"
and you remember how life was
and you see
how it is today.
I feel... the hurt of a former Staff Sergeant M.P.
when he is told he is a half inch
too short for a civilian police force.
I feel...your hurt as a man dies when he runs his car
under your truck and your job is lost
because your truck
is parked at the
local...
beer...
garden...

We
don't

talk.

Daddy I can't see hear feel you,
save for dry recollection.
Is it the alcohol that I see drain
your soul away like so much water
in a pay toilet,
or is it the scars of teasing
I took when I was young
and all the children knew
that my father was drunk again,
or was it spilled sheet cake on Clarence's birthday?
Even then I perceived...
knew...
saw,
that your hurt was deeper than ours,
but young boys are so unforgiving of
unperfected fathers.

You say
we
don't
talk
I think it's rather we can't talk.
There is a wall within
that I have not let Jesus
break down
and when out of your need
you told me
you loved me
the wall came up
and would not
let me
speak.
We will talk,
I mean really talk,
but today all that I have

to offer...
I offer
right now.

In the name of Jesus
I claim our healing,
and I love you.
I always have.
Forgive me
please
forgive me.

Restoration

(In three Poems)

Conviction

Aloneness covers you blanket like-cold.
There are many lies but the one
you struggle hardest not to believe
is that you are utterly forsaken,
unloved by God or man.

Hold on
          fellowship
                    embrace the word and…
hold on!

Hope

You believe that God
is with you. You know
that you have help,
and at the far end
of the cold moss-covered tunnel
there is now the promise
of light.

Move forward
          lift your head
                    strengthen your back
and…
move forward!

Deliverance

There is light.
Light that fills every aspect
of your life, every pore of your being,

the light of deliverance.
You add to it with rejoicing and
praise, and are lifted to gossamer
heights and joy unspeakable.

Your restoration is at hand,
even when you think
you have fallen beyond help

hold on
        move forward
                        for…
your restoration
is at hand!

On Seeking Enlightenment

Back in the day when
I was seeking enlightenment
I kept my ear to the ground listening
for all the newest and deepest ideas.

I could quote you the top five physical
and spiritual reasons why you shouldn't eat pork.

I conversed freely about some who have thirty-three
degrees of knowledge and others who have three hundred
and sixty degrees.

I read every book on Zen from "Zen in the Art of
Archery" to "Zen in the Art of Motorcycle Maintenance."

I could converse about politics, mysticism and jazz all in
the same paragraph and still maintain
that philosophical deep look.

I applauded the musicians that performed life's questions
as though they had all the answers.

I read from Oliver Wendell Holms to St Augustine and
made them all fit into my unique little philosophy of life.

I would quote things like, "If one asked of the truth and
another told him you can be sure that neither had
knowledge about the nature of truth."

I had the respect of all the hip cats and heavy dudes who
could likewise philosophize with the best of them.

I, with my fellow sophist, were led into deep
complexities,

that I took for simplicities, and a detailed exploration
of my own natural instincts.

Yet in all of this there was always
something missing. Even when the social,
political and philosophical thing fit snugly
together there was this unexplainable vacantness.

It would seem that the whole was less
than the sum of all those individual parts.

Then, like a salmon returning to its birth stream
I returned to my early training,
namely my mother's relationship with God.
Her midnight prayers her sincere faith
was like a beacon that provided warm memories
of strength, peace and precious contentment.

Then early one morning
not far from Damascus road
the scales fell from my eyes.

Now one surrender, one baptism
And one filling of the Holy Spirit later
I can say the truth,
the whole truth and
nothing but the truth
in three words
three times and
in three seconds.

Jesus is Lord!
Jesus is Lord!
Jesus is Lord!

Invitation

The fire roared in love and power,
And from the bush proclaimed the hour
That salvation now was close at hand,
And the Lord himself would make the stand.

Holy fire,
Eternal fire,
Fire of healing,
Fire of cleansing,

The Lord our God will baptize you with fire.
The fire calls and burns and moves,
To reach the lost and proclaim the news
That all who see they will receive.
The fire burns eternally.

Holy fire,
Eternal fire,
Fire of healing,
Fire of cleansing,

The lord our God will baptize you with fire.
The fire burns away the fake
With power that can surly make
A new life that he freely gives,
Come now partake of God and live.

Holy fire,
Eternal fire,
Fire of healing,
Fire of cleansing,

The Lord our God will baptize you with fire.

What I Have Come To Know

(For my sisters, a journey to psalm 91:1)

When I came to know
That he did not love me now
My sun grew dim
Graying a daily walk
That I no longer chose to lift
Into the joy of believing God
And all my times swirled downward
Into a numb and cold existence

When I came to know
That he never did love me
I embraced an empty promise
With desperate gifts of flesh
(I was a useful fool)
My gifts could make him love me
I believed this in my head
Though my heart had told me no

When I came to know
That he was cruel and would not love me
I stumbled down and wept
For my love had been impossible
Another self-delusion
Mirage of thirsty soul

When I came to know
The pain of a lonely heart
Anger and hardness took me
So, I played the familiar game
Trading flesh for lying affections
Living a life of need
In desperate compromise
Showing all a clown's painted smile

Hiding even from myself

But

When I came to know
That I was really loved of Jesus
I dwelled in His secret place
He wiped away my tears
And called me His beloved
I no longer played the game
Smiling falsely as a clown

This love in His secret place
I had never known before
In peace I was brightly covered
Lighting my daily walk
And lifting it on high

When I came to know
That all I need is Jesus
And the plans He has for me
Are for good and not for evil
For He has the man who loves me
Seeking diligently for me
When I have been prepared
This man He has will find me

I rest now in the promise
And joy of believing God
This is the secret place
That I have come to know

Haiku Definitions

Poiema (Workmanship) (Eph2:10)

Crafted expression
of God. We are his love poem,
wooing wayward world.

Grace (Heb 12:28)

God's love expressed as
personality; working
in, for, and through us.

Holiness (Rom 12:1)

Escapes perfection's
hopelessness by living
body sacrifice.

Faith (Hab 2:4)

Saying yes when your
will, intellect, emotion,
say no to your God.

Sons of God (1John 3:1-3)

God's genderless term
of endearment, bequeathing
our role in the earth.

Christmas Haiku

His birth ascends through
crimsoned dark walled tomorrow.
Let all earth rejoice.

Thoughts and Ruminations

1
A Mother is angry. This mother's son is attending a church of another denomination. Her son and a boy from this other church met at school and became friends. Her son enjoys the other church more than the one he grew up in. She does not trust that other church. If she fails, her son may become a passionate witness for Christ at that other church. If she fails, her son will not necessarily be shot.

Another mother is angry. Her son refuses to attend any church, anywhere, at any time. If she fails, her son may be shot in a drive by shooting.

In this way, their worlds are different.

2
God is not a good fortune teller, He does not look into the future, He does not look into the past. God sees and abides in all time at the same time. God lives in the infinite present, which is eternity, as well as every part of the linear progression known as time. Therefore God sees all of time and everything that has and will happen much like we look at a map of the world. God sees the beginning and end of great roads of history, boarders of change, intersections of conflict and more. The most important to him are small, short side streets.
Your life is a small, short side street.

3
Pharisees, Sadducees, and Teachers of the Law have taught us many lessons. One of the most important lessons are that religion and or religious culture can live separate from, antagonistic to or even the enemy of the

life of Christ.

Many churches continue this lesson today.

4
When we first come to God, he follows us and is with us always, no matter where we go or what we do he loves us and ever desires to be closer to us and bless us. In all things he was crucified for us.

Then things may change.

If our love for God becomes deep enough, we follow him and are with him always. No matter where he goes or what he does we love him and are ever desiring to be a blessing to him. In all things we are crucified with him.

The second way is more excellent than the first, I think.

5
A pastor must grow his church. He recruits Christians from other churches. He recruits people from the world in which he is familiar. He studies the latest business models.

He drives past the crack house every day.

They are not good recruits neither are they mentioned in his business model. They have not been invited. They are in very good company. The spirit of God has also not been invited.

6
I once owned a dog that was known as a fear biter. Fear biters are dogs that are insecure and therefore always intimidated by people and other dogs. This makes them unnecessarily dangerous and destructive because they

will attack innocent people and dogs based on their own unwarranted fears. These dogs always feel vulnerable and threatened even when no threats exist. They are especially dangerous when facing the unfamiliar or something they do not understand. A fear biter that perceives a nonexistent threat will attack viciously to protect itself and its territory.

Note to self: I must always and in every way endeavor to be better than a frightened dog.

7
Christians, the really good ones, know better than and therefore, take great care not to be associated with, be seen in the company of, or risk their reputation with the sexually immoral, drunkards, thieves or anyone else of ill repute. In this way Christians, the really good ones, know better than Jesus, who had the unfortunate circumstance of being called the friend of tax collectors and sinners.

8
Augustine is intelligent. Augustine has studied many books for many years and has many answers. One of Augustine's answers are if there is a God at best, he can only be understood through a complicated philosophical journey and at worst is unknowable. Augustine is not aware that he and his books have found many answers, but that none of these answers spring from the correct questions. Many years later, Augustine has become St Augustine and he says,

"Understanding is the reward
of faith. So, seek not to understand that you may believe but believe that you may understand."

In this statement we see that St Augustine has learned the most important question and its answer.

9
The enemy of all souls works hard to shape this world in his image. The enemy of all souls also works very hard to disguise his hand in this shaping. This world provides more food than is needed but people go hungry. This world provides more land than is needed but we have war. This world kills adults and children with preventable diseases. This world provides humans with opportunities and training to perform limitless forms of wickedness and cruelty from our early life to our death bed. In all the history of humanity we have never been able to slow, much less stop, this systematic degradation.

The world as OZ…

Please pay attention to the mind behind the curtain.

10
See our God. He is laughing loudly. He is laughing in heaven and he is also here on earth. The nations are very angry. They are so angry that they point their water guns at God and squeeze the trigger. He laughs even more. The nations go into a rage. They call our God rude. They say that to laugh while someone is trying to disbelieve you is extremely impolite. They threaten to disbelieve him more and also, to shoot him again. This makes God hysterical. He almost doubles over with laughter.

The nations have imagined a vain thing. They have imagined that to disbelieve God is to make him not exist. So, they wave their water guns violently and disbelieve harder. This makes God slap his knee and vibrate laughing. Our God is laughing. Our God who longs to be their God is laughing.

Our God is laughing to keep from crying.

Mixed Nuts

We all live suspended in the narrow
space between one heartbeat and eternity.

Oh God! Are you out there?!?!
No… I'm here with you.

I am soaked, proof that the rain falls on the just and the unjust. Proof that circumstance won't tell
me which one I am.

The Christian Equation:
(Jesus + relationship) x Love = Lifestyle

I claw at my Christian mask hoping to find underneath some expression of Jesus.

Text from God:
You said OMG...Am I Really?

Biblical Tabloid:
Goliath was slung down in a run by stoning in the valley today by young David for dissing his peeps and their God.

Twenty First Century Repentance:
I have just killed Uriah and plan to marry Bathsheba. Solution: I will never fail to attend church on Mother's Day again.

Note to Self:
You can pray on an airplane or you can read the emergency instructions on an airplane but apparently doing both at the same time really freaks people out

Text from God:
I don't exist?!! LOL

Televangelist to Audience:
"Do I look like a man who could be trusted to provide your weekly loan shark?"

When I tell you I am Christian you pause
and I begin to glimpse the mob with their torches.

Note to Self:
We walk by faith and not by sight, but God still expects you to look both ways before you cross the street.

A beautiful day, the birds are chirping, the bees are humming, the people are marrying and giving in marriage…and the clock is ticking.

Paradox:
God knows me completely.
God loves me completely.

Text from God:
HIT ME BACK!!!

"You need Jesus!" is a universal truth, not a left-handed insult of character.

Children's Haiku
Jesus rules, devil
drools. Jesus is fun for me.
Loves like mom and dad.

Other Radical Explorations

Parable

There was once a kingdom who sometimes forgot what they were born to do. They forgot too often and remembered too slowly.

One day their forgetfulness was seen in the fear of a giant who made his stand in the middle of a valley. This giant stood daily in the middle of the valley for the shadow of valleys is where giants wax strong and defied the courage of the forgetful kingdom. The kingdom shrank back from the defying giant for they feared to try and slay such as he and they feared to walk through the valley of shadow.

There was once a young poet who was charged by his father to take courage alone in faraway valleys. He was charged by his father to kill lion and bear with only such tools as a poet might have. So, he learned to trust his father's command when he was alone and no one else saw.

One day this poet was sent by his father to the valley of Elah to strengthen his brothers and he saw the giant yet defying the kingdom and his anger was kindled and he said aloud; "Who is this giant to defy this kingdom, a kingdom well able to slay such as he. For my father I killed both lion and bear this giant will be like one of these!"

He went forth with the tools to kill lion and bear, only such tools as a poet might have. He did not fear the valley of shadow, for he had walked through valleys before, and he slew the giant like the lion and bear with the unimpressive tools of his father's command.

The forgetful kingdom saw this and then they remembered that they were well able to slay such as he and they feared no longer the valley of shadow and in their new courage they charged boldly forward and won a great victory for then they remembered that this is what they were born to do.
Such is the Father's call of a Christian poet.

Nature of Light

He is the King eternal, immortal, invisible.
Light is invisible. We cannot see light. We can only see what light touches and illuminates. The evidence that light is present is always and only the things light touches and illuminates. Outer space between our planet and the sun is full of sunlight, but it is dark. We cannot see this light. If we see a planet or a space craft or any object in space, then we see the evidence of the light that is always present, as the light illuminates the object that we see. Outer space is dark because it is a vacuum. It is a vast emptiness, and there is nothing in this vacuum or emptiness for light to touch and illuminate. If light cannot find anything to touch and illuminate, then there is darkness. Light will never cease to be light but if there is nothing it can touch then we will live in darkness and not perceive the light that is everywhere.

You are the light of the world.

Pure light contains all colors. These colors are in harmony and are not separate in pure light. Pure light can be fractured into a rainbow. This is the separation and deformity of the nature of pure light. Rainbow light is fractured and is very poor at touching and illuminating. Rainbow light does not reveal the true nature of things because each part of the rainbow is lacking every other part of itself. When a particular part of rainbow light touches something the illumination is tainted by its own color. A particular part of a rainbow colors everything after the nature of its own color therefore it does not reveal the true nature of the thing it touches. This is the difference between unified light and fractured light.

Unified light reveals what is true, fractured light shows us only after its own color.

I*n him was life; and that life was the light of men.*

Light is necessary for life. If the world had no light, every living thing would die, and nothing new would be born. Light gives life to every living thing, and, every living thing receives its life from light. If the world no longer had light, every plant and every animal would die. Even animals that live in total darkness and are blind ignoring and living as if there was no light, would die because everything that sustains them, everything they depend on, even though they are unaware of it, is sustained by light.

For He is the Lord, He does not change.

Light is not relative. Light does not change according to your perspective or from what place you observe it. Light travels at 299,792,458 meters per second in a vacuum and is observed at that speed from every perspective. If a car travels at 100 miles per hour and you travel next to that car at 75 miles per hour that car you are beside will only appear to pass you at 25 miles per hour. The car is traveling 25 miles per hour faster than you so its relative speed to you is 25 miles per hour. For light this is not so. If you travel extremely fast, even approaching the speed of light itself light will still appear to you to be traveling at 299,792'458 meters per second. Time and space will change around you to allow light to appear to you this way. Light does not change; it doesn't matter from where you observe it.

Light overcomes darkness.

Darkness cannot exist of its own but only in the absence of light. When light touches anything then darkness disappears. Darkness cannot overcome light and darken what light touches. Darkness can only cover something in the absence of light. Darkness cannot be measured. There is no speed of darkness. Darkness does not travel in waves or particles. Darkness does not have mass or energy. Darkness only exists and moves in the absence of something for light to touch. Light and darkness are not equally powerful. They do not compete with one another. Light's mere existence moves the darkness into nonexistence. Light has no competition. Darkness is only the absence of light.

And the light shines in the darkness but the darkness did not comprehend it.

Light takes every opportunity to have access. Great pains have to be taken to exclude light and cultivate darkness. Light will take every opportunity, move through every crack or seem, to touch and illuminate. Light is also gentle. It will not force its way. If darkness is sought it can always be found. Dark places can be found or created away from the light because light will not force its way, but if light is carried into the dark place it will cease to be a dark place. That place will have light. To stay in darkness, you must actively seek or create dark places and flee when light is brought to that dark place. It takes decisive action to stay in darkness. Light takes every given opportunity to touch and illuminate. Light constantly seeks to eliminate darkness but light is gentle it will not force its way.

God is light and in him is no darkness at all.

Yes, God is light. As we understand the nature of physical light, we can begin to understand the nature of God who is spiritual light. God touches and illuminates. God unifies us as the light of the world and God's heart is broken when we are fractured from one another. God provides life and without God all flesh would die together. God does not change. God is the same yesterday, today, and forever. God overcomes darkness. Darkness has no power over God. Darkness exists in man because of God's mercy. God is always seeking to touch and illuminate the human heart. God will use even the smallest opportunity to touch us but God will not force his way.

Atheist Faith

I think I do not have enough faith to be an atheist. You see, I asked my friend the atheist why the universe is ordered. For example, why are the laws of physics constant when there is no scientific reason why they should be? Things in a vacuum fall to the earth at 32ft per second per second every time. Why wouldn't it fall 32ft per second per second one time and 4ft per second per second the next? It seems that in physics and everywhere else we look we find an imposed order, an unexplained uniformity.

My friend told me that the universe is not ordered but chaotic and that random variables come together to cause a constant rate of fall. Things fall at the same rate on earth because the earth displaces a constant amount of space, and causes a constant amount of gravity which results in the consistency of the fall. If you change any of the variables the rate of the fall will change. Order is the illusion of chaotic variables.

I told my friend that we should not be like the fish that cannot see what water is because it cannot see what water is not. The fish does not know what water is because it has always been surrounded by water and cannot imagine a world outside of water. It is hard for us to see what order is because we have never seen what order is not. We have always been surrounded by order.

There is no scientific reason why any law of physics should behave the same way twice. Just because we have always observed these laws behaving consistently and have even worked out science based on these observations does not mean there is a scientific reason why they should. Humans had always observed things fall to the earth, but it was not until Sir Isaac Newton asked why that we began to explore the concept of gravity.

To date there is no scientific reason why the earth would displace a constant amount of space, why gravity would cause a constant pull and cause a thing to fall at a constant rate. All of these variables that come together are separate pieces of the same order. Whenever any of these variables or any law of physics behaves the same way constantly, it is obeying an imposed order and there is no scientific explanation for why it should.

My friend told me that every indication is that the universe has always functioned this way since very shortly after the big bang and that there is an answer and one day science will discover it.

I then asked my friend the atheist what caused the big bang and what came before it.

He then explained to me that there are many theories about the big bang and the origin of the universe, but the most important idea for me to grasp is that time was probability created at the big bang as a part of our universe, so that our universe and time share the same beginning, and time is possibly limited to the outer edge of our finite universe as it expands. So, there was technically no before the big bang since time did not exist.

I was not satisfied though and asked him if these various theories explained what caused time to suddenly appear out of eternity through the big bang.

He told me that string theory, and its multiple dimensions can explain where time came from, and possibly what happened before it.

So, I asked why the dimensions explained by string theory suddenly create time and all the matter and energy in our universe through the big bang.

He then told me that there is a limit to how far back we can see and how much we can understand at this time, because life and mankind has only existed for a short time in our universe, not long enough to grasps everything from the start to finish.

So, then I asked my friend the atheist how life came into existence. He then explained to me about the primordial pool, amino acid strings, solar ultraviolet energy and other things that seemed really scientific and important.

That did not answer my question though. I wanted to know how an inanimate object becomes alive. How can a group of inanimate chemicals like amino acids that have no consciousness become animated and evolve a rudimentary survival instinct and begin to respond to its environment enough to do what is necessary to stay alive.

He explained to me about life precursors and DNA instructions in the most basic forms of life, but told me that we did not yet know, and that one-day science would give us an explanation.

So, then I asked my friend the atheist how something as complex as DNA, could have been constructed randomly. It is hard to accept that billions of possible bases came together in exactly the correct sequence to create just the right nucleotides, and that these nucleotides out of all the possible alternatives would connect in perfect order to form the exact working twisted double helix DNA strands to accidentally create sustainable life.

My friend told me that anything was possible given enough time and number of attempts. He then stated that a good way for me to understand this concept is the "Infinite Monkey Theorem." Simply put, this theorem states that mathematically if you have an infinite number of typewriters typed by an infinite number of monkeys, one of those monkeys would produce perfectly the complete works of Shakespeare. He said that no matter how complex something is, it can be randomly produced given the right set of circumstances.

I did not think his analogy was relevant since he had previously told me that this version of the expanding universe was finite in time and space, which means it would not allow infinite time or attempts. This means that he would have to have a finite group of monkeys with a finite number of typewriters, which changes his analogy.

When you have an infinite number of anything, the math becomes completely different from math that does not deal with the infinite. For instance, if he gave me thirty percent of his infinite monkeys and typewriters, I would soon realize that I too had an infinite number of monkeys and typewriters and he would still have an infinite number of monkeys and typewriters, even though he had just given me thirty percent of his.

Infinity is a concept but does not exist in time or space. There is not an infinite amount of anything. In the realm of the finite however, even one monkey on one typewriter for every particle of the observable universe (ten to the eightieth power) typing one thousand key strokes per second for one hundred times the scientifically believed age of the universe (ten to the twentieth power) the chance of these monkeys creating any large part of any work of Shakespeare, not to mention the complete works, is just about impossible (approaches zero).

I also thought it was odd that he would use intelligent beings in his theorem, even if the intelligence of the monkeys did not approach Shakespeare's intelligence. It seems to me that any type of intelligence would pollute the outcome.

I thought a better analogy would be a finite number of tornadoes in a finite number of automobile factories creating a working car which is even less likely than his finite typing monkey theorem. He did not seem to like my tornado car theorem very much and told me that mere statistical mathematics, as it pertained to creation was not enough to shake his disbelief in God creating life.

I then told him that I thought all his answers lacked the same thing, a first cause. I told him that I knew what the first cause was. He was not extremely interested and told me that he would hold on to his beliefs, as they were and one day if I really thought about it and was honest with myself that I would come to believe as he did.

Now that is great faith!

The Ant That Would Be King

Take a mind trip with me. No, not a drug induced purple haze mind trip mind you, but a mind trip induced from fresh air and a searching heart. A mind trip can be useless, or we can learn something from it. You decide which type of mind trip this one is.

Imagine that ants from your backyard garden have invaded your house and what they don't know is that they are only days away from the exterminator. These ants were content to live in your backyard garden with all its juicy fruits and vegetables until a new leader ant from another anthill put himself in charge of the ants from your backyard. This ant knows just a little more than the other ants do, and this ant doesn't want the ants to dig and aerate your soil or guard the garden from harmful insects. This ant has gone as far as to believe he should be in charge of the house and has convinced the other ants that they should have all those goodies from your kitchen.

The question is, how could we save these ants from the exterminator? Could we post a danger sign? No, a sign wouldn't help an ant. Could we seal the house? No, ants can always find a way into the house and therefore into death. If we spoke to the ants at the top of our voice would that help? No, ants couldn't begin to understand sound as language.

It seems that these ants are doomed.

The problem is ants don't live on our level. They couldn't even begin to understand a fraction of what we know. You couldn't teach an ant sound as language because they communicate by chemicals. If an ant is in danger it releases a chemical that whips the other ants into a frenzy to fight. If an ant finds food, it releases a chemical that says food is found. The ant mind is small and limited to extremely basic things. You couldn't teach an ant to use a cell phone, to write poetry or to convey even simple ideas like yes or no to his fellow ants. You can't teach an ant any of the most basic things that you do every day. It is, beyond them. To make things worse, the ant from the other anthill speaks their language. This ant has released a food chemical trail leading right into your kitchen. The ants from your backyard don't know what else to do so they follow the trail strait to their future destruction.

There is one thing that you can do though. You can become an ant yourself. It is really the only way to save them. If you, a human, become an ant you would still understand about exterminators and kitchens and could help the ants live. No, you still couldn't explain everything to the ants because it would still be beyond them to understand. What you could do because you are now an ant as well as human is speak at their level by releasing your own chemical that would lead them back to the backyard garden. The ants would have to follow your path only because they had faith in you and what you communicated to them they could not rely on their limited understanding.

No doubt the ant from the other anthill would try and stop you because he would fight to stay in control of the ants. That ant would release an attack chemical to the other ants whenever you and the ants that follow you are around. This would whip those other ants into a frenzy and cause them to try and kill you and the ants that follow you. The more you and your followers release the chemical of the path back to the garden the more the ant from the other anthill would try to have you killed, but more and more ants would still begin to follow you. Even some of the ants that were tricked into trying to kill you would become some of your faithful followers.

Alas that deceiving ant would think that if he killed you that the battle would be over. So, it would only be a matter of time before you would be killed. Your followers though would continue to communicate to the other ants to follow the path you started, and every ant that followed that path would end up back in the garden with all the delicious fruit. The good news for you would be that even when you are killed by the unbelieving ants you would still be human. Only your ant body would die, and since your ant body was from your human body you could bring your ant body back, and because you would have power over your ant life you would have power over any ant life so that all those ants that were killed following your path you could bring back and place them in the garden.

And that old ant from the other anthill days would be numbered because once you were back to yourself you could have the exterminator deal with him whenever you wanted to. You wouldn't do it right away of course, because you would want as many of the deceived ants to come to follow your path as would come. After all you wouldn't want the deceived ants to die along with the ant from another anthill without having an opportunity to choose the right path and live.

That's it, the end of the mind trip. Now that we are done I just have two questions.

Number 1- Was this mind trip useless?
Number 2 - Can anyone help me understand why God had to become a man called Jesus?

Harry Potter VS the Ku Klux Klan

Some Christians are offended by Harry Potter. They say that because Harry practices witchcraft they cannot help but be offended. It would be something different, they say, if there was no such thing as real witchcraft but since there are real witches trying to war against humanity a witch, who is a hero, is offensive. I haven't had time to think about it much myself because I have been working on my own idea...

I am creating a character called Parry Hotter who is in training to be a grand wizard of the Ku Klux Klan. I know what you're thinking. You're thinking that this character would be offensive, and people would not want to see him because being a Klansman can never be seen in a positive light.

Well, that's where you're wrong.

My young Klansman is not one of the bigoted bad Klansman, but my Klansman uses his skills for good. For instance: Parry does not burn crosses on the lawns of minorities, but he burns his crosses on the lawns of the bad bigoted Klansman. He puts on his white sheet and hood to terrorize these bad Klansman and drive them away to keep the minority's safe. When these bad Klansman refuse to leave and minorities remain in danger, then Parry must go to the next level and he and his friends show up in the middle of the night at the bad Klansman's home and spirit them off and these bad Klansman will never be seen or heard of again.

We must keep in mind that Parry was forced to take this drastic action because the bad Klansman are so evil and bad that they left poor young Parry with no other choice.

You should also keep in mind that young Parry is really harmless, to the general public anyway, and is also so cute and innocent looking that no one could possibility be offended by him.

My character Parry Hotter should be no more offensive to the general public than Harry Potter is to Christians because when you are fighting evil, and very cute, whatever you are and whatever techniques you use can never be offensive. Right...?

A Rabbi, A Priest and A Minister Walk Into A Bar…

A rabbi, a priest and a minister walk into a bar. The bartender looks up and says, "What's this, some kind of joke." Rim shot, cymbal crash!

Maybe it is some kind of joke, but should it be? The idea that a Godly leader has things, situations, and places that he or she is above only serves to make such leadership irrelevant to the society that he or she should be serving. The perception that a bartender would be someone better to talk to about real-life issues than a Godly leader is only possible when that leader feels above the people. Godly leadership disconnected from the people is the greatest of contradictions because it is also Godly leadership disconnected from God.

Jesus was in so called inappropriate settings and with inappropriate people so often he was called a drunkard and a friend of sinners. In fact, you would be hard pressed to find where Jesus spoke a harsh word to any sinner except religious leaders. Jesus got involved in the lives of people in a positive way no matter what they had done or where they were. It is unfortunate but there are very many people who mistakenly feel that if Jesus met them, he would never associate with them and he certainly would never do it in a bar.

Throughout history when Godly leadership is more devoted to their religious status within a society than to serving the people through God we find the most horrible crimes against people committed in the name of Christ. The seed for the horrors of the Spanish Inquisition where planted with the fertilizer of notions of superiority.

If we are honest, we will agree that there have always been two groups that claimed to follow God. One in agreement with the world and living according to the principles of the world, and the other following God through his Word. Everything from Cain slaying his brother Abel to any present-day religious violence and oppression is due to the worldly religion. The self-sacrifice, charity and unwillingness to see themselves above others are given to us from a Godly relationship.

There have been times in history where worldly religion has oppressed Godly relationship and there have been times when the lines have blurred between them. The important question for all of us is which group has given us our perception of God and therefore shaped how we live our lives?

If Jesus walked into a bar would the bartender think that it was the start of a joke or would he know that a bar would be one of Jesus's hangouts? Would the people in that bar know that Jesus was not there to look down on them but to hang out and offer them life?

The Atheist and the Train

I was telling my friend the atheist a story. As it turns out, he didn't like my story and I don't know why. Maybe you can help me figure it out. The story I told my friend the the atheist went like this.

Once upon a time there was a good politician who got a great idea at the train platform on his way to work. Every day he would talk to a homeless man that would come to the platform to beg for change. He would give the man money and after finding out that the man was dying from an incurable liver disease caused from drinking and drug use he felt he had to do something for the people in the city who were homeless and suffering.

He would call it the Phoenix Initiative.

On this particular day the good politician was in the midst of a crisis. It had taken him five years to bring together, politicians, businessmen, educators, community leaders and public opinion to bring about the Phoenix Initiative. Tens of thousands of people would be helped and the entire city would be uplifted not just in the short term, but for generations. Many times, his dream to help the city looked like it would die but the good politician was always able to save the day with his skill as a negotiator and his ability to make people believe that we can help one another and create a better world to live in.

This time it looked like even the skills of the good politician could not save the day. The good politician would not give up though. After a week and a half of phone calls and impromptu meetings it looked like he might yet pull it out. One last person had to be brought back on board so, he changed into his suit on a Saturday afternoon with his phone to his ear and raced out of the door. He was not able to convince this last person over the phone, but he knew if he met with them in person, he could convince them to do the right thing. The good politician tied his tie as he ran the two blocks to the train which was the only way he could make it to this person before they left for Europe on business.

The good politician got to the train platform just in time. The train would be there in two or three minutes. He could already see it in the distance. Then a horrible revelation invaded his brain. He had rushed out so quickly that when he changed clothes, he didn't change his wallet into his suit pocket. It was at home in his jeans. He had no way of paying for the train. He would miss the last meeting and the Phoenix Initiative would be dead. All he could think was that tens of thousands of people would suffer because he was absent minded.

Just then he saw the homeless man passed out in the gutter just off the platform and the sight of him sharpened the pain of his impending failure. Then a sudden idea gave him a sliver of hope. He shook the homeless man to ask him for his wine money. Not only did the homeless man say no, but he said he would be dead in a month or so, and he didn't care what happened after he was gone. He also told the good politician to shut up and go away or he would cut him with his knife. The homeless man then rolled over in the gutter and passed out once more.

The good politician was undaunted. He took a large stone that was lying nearby and lifted it high above his head. The good politician paused for a second and then smashed the stone down on the homeless man's head. While the homeless man's legs where still twitching, he took his wine money from his pocket and it was just enough to pay for his train. The good politician made his train and his meeting. The Phoenix Initiative was resurrected, and tens of thousands of people where helped, and the city was uplifted for generations to come.

The End.

My atheist Friend thought that it was a horrible story. Apparently, he thought that the actions of the good politician were less than admirable to say the least. Our conversation went something like this.

My atheist friend: It is wrong to murder someone for any reason let alone train fare.

Confused me: But many more lives would be saved because of his actions.

My atheist Friend: You can't arbitrarily take a human life just because you think it serves the greater good.

Confused me: Why not, if there is no God.

My atheist friend- Don't be ridiculous. If we do not hold to a human standard of goodness, we are doomed. We don't need a creator God to believe that.

Confused me- This is exactly my point. As humans we must choose for the greater good. If you believe life is an accidental combination of inert materials from a primordial soup, then the only value it has is what we assign to it. The homeless man was not ever going to contribute to the greater good. The homeless man had been chosen by evolution to perish because of his illness. There was no way to assign value to his life outside of every life being sacred because it is a gift from God. So, if there is no God, then the greater good was for him to die and for thousands of others to be helped.

My atheist friend: You are confused and obviously unable to understand the most basic tenants of a secular humanistic philosophy as it pertains to the good of mankind.

Confused me: That's strange, your last statement sounded like what has been said by many people throughout history that destroyed human life for what they perceived as the greater good. Are you sure you don't like my story?

My atheist friend then stormed off. He still couldn't explain to me why he didn't like my story, but I think I may have figured it out. I think it is simply this, what we sometimes believe in theory is quite different when we see it in practice. What is scary to me is that we don't usually discover this until it is too late.

Lesson

That woman Jezebel who calls herself a prophetess was violently attacking the preachers of God. She attacked God's preachers by telling the people that the preachers knew not the love of their God. She then told God's people that because their God loved them, he did not require a holy lifestyle. Her plan is always to seduce the people teaching them all to worship their flesh.

She rose up false preachers to support all her teaching and lead most away from the Word of their God. The false teachers taught that sin would not hurt them and to sin in their flesh was acceptable to God. So, God sent to them a drought and a famine to warn all his people of serving their flesh. The people ignored God's sovereign warning for the flesh has its pleasure and people will serve it though painful and violent and wicked it is. They did not believe that their God was yet willing to search hearts and minds and then judge their flesh. The Word to them had become without meaning since Jezebel taught that God could be mocked.

Then God sent a preacher to speak to the people and teach them a lesson of the power of His Word. The preacher stood at the top of Mount Carmel and said, "Serve God's Word or trust in your flesh!" The people stood tall and silent before him for God was not feared, they feared only flesh.

The preacher then challenged all the false preachers to call on the flesh to heal and deliver. The false preachers preached from morning to evening but nothing miraculous happened for them. The preacher then preached the Word of his Father and the Father moved with fire and power and the people were changed and trusted God's Word and moved the false preachers away from their lives. The father then sent them rain and provision and the people were

healed, and the people were delivered, and the people rejoiced in the love of their God.

Such is the preacher's battle with the flesh.

Prodigals

It came to pass that the men from man came before the prophet seeking to question him and justify themselves before him.

And so, it was that the first man from man came forward and said: "I am moral and most religious. Therefore I ask you this prophet; why do you say that God loves the poor in spirit when we all know that unless someone lives as well as we do, they will not see heaven?"

The prophet then said: "Man from man I have something to say to you." and the man from man said, "Say on!" The prophet then said, "The words of your own mouth testify against you for God has not called us to morality but to Holiness. Holiness is God's standard for life for those who love Him. This standard grows out of the relationship he has with his people. Morality is humanity's ever-changing standard to justify itself before God and the world around us.

God has also not called us to religion but to salvation. Religion is humanity's attempt to reach God through its own ability but salvation is God's specific plan to reconcile lost humanity to him. But as for your question; the poor in spirit know that they are in need and therefore are rich but those who consider themselves rich in spirit are self-sufficient and therefore poor. Now go find the meaning of these words; 'I desire mercy and not sacrifice."

Then the man from man fell back in the dust with much weeping and gnashing of teeth.

The next man from man came forward and said: "I am

Marx, and I say that you make claims that God makes us all free but in reality, humanity has been made slaves, chained in a capitalistic environment where they are alienated and estranged from themselves and others. All of your claims that God improves our lives are simply lies to lull us into complacency so that we can be more easily controlled. Your teachings are nothing more than the opiate of the masses."

And the prophet answered him and said: "You foolish blind guide! You profess to see clearly but it is your own blind arrogance that is destroying you. Yours is the sin committed at the tower of Babel, yours is the hardness of heart that Judas and many others have shown God. Like Babel you are trying to elevate your life without God. Like Judas you only see the things outside of the human heart, humanity's carnal needs and environment.

You are blind to what God offers though he stands before you day after day. You fail to see that it is not humanity's environment or need that brings about evil, but it is the condition of sin. You can change every person's environment into what you consider the perfect utopia, but wickedness will still prevail until you can free us all from the fallen condition of sin. Every society from the very beginning contained violence and degradation. Even so-called innocent humans living in remote rain forest away from a capitalistic system, and with relatively plentiful resources all around them commit murder, steal, and lie. You can't see that God has destroyed the power of sin and called men to a quality life. In this present world, the freedom that God gives is the only utopia possible with perfection
attained in the world to come.

As for the rest of your claims; you have seen people come in God's name claiming to be of God. These are ravenous wolves, clouds without rain, which walk in a form of Godliness but deny the power thereof. They have deceived some and murdered others. These are what you call the opiate of the masses. You fail to see the most obvious opiate which is sin and the blindness that sin brings. God's words are true no matter how many liars who pretend to be of God enter the world. God is your only way to true freedom, therefore repent or your destruction in the coming tribulation is sure."

The second man from man fell back in the dust with much weeping and gnashing of teeth.

Then the next man from man came forward and said, "I am a spiritual being reaching for a higher spiritual plane and I see that your teaching doesn't include all that it should. How can your followers reach a higher spiritual plane when they eat meat and break many other laws written in their own bodies?"

The Prophet said: "You have been blinded by the basic principles of this world. You can't see that it is not what goes in a person's mouth but what comes out that defiles them. You live by instinct always learning but never able to accept the truth. You, like the Pharisees of old, think, that you can be justified spiritually by your own works. This is impossible. It is by God's grace through faith only that you can reach a higher spiritual plane. This is God's gift to you.

Yours is a doctrine of the physical not the spiritual. Even if you followed the laws of your body in the strictest sense your spiritual righteousness would be like filthy rags. When you stay in bed one half second longer than God intended a human to stay in bed you are a sluggard. If you eat one half teaspoonful more food than God intended a human to eat, you are a glutton. You fail to see that sin is your condition not things that you choose to do. You can never trust your instincts and intuition to lead you to a higher spiritual plane for all of humanity's nature was warped at Eden.

I tell you the truth, when you follow all of your natural laws you will still only live three score and ten years or four score if you have the strength then you will die. Your physical laws have no power over death. God has given us the way and the truth and the life, no one comes to God the father but by his son Jesus who is Christ. Your only hope to escape death and move to a higher spiritual plane is through the simple plan of salvation, which is justification through Jesus Christ, yet you do not believe in him, so you stand condemned already. Go now and understand the meaning of this saying; 'You must be born again."

And the man from man fell back in the dust with much weeping and gnashing of teeth.

The next man from man came forward and said: "I am the atheist. I believe that there can't be a God who would allow all this pain and suffering in the world and furthermore, a loving God would not punish people with an eternal hell for making mistakes in this meaningless life." The prophet then said; "It is yours to believe: If you do not believe today you will have no choice but to believe it on that day.

As for your statement, when humanity surrendered its authority to the enemy through Adam in Eden the enemy became the prince of this world in our stead and sin resulted. All of creation is warped and cursed by sin and the resulting pain and death comes from the enemy of all creation. Through our own authority, our enemy deceives us into twisting and warping the system of the world. The pain and suffering you speak of is all of us acting on the deceptive direction given. No wickedness can exist without the authority of a participating human being. It is through Christ that we can again take up our God given authority and destroy the wickedness that we find and bring what is good and loving into the world.

As for sending people to hell for making mistakes, God will send no one to hell. Hell was not prepared for the souls of men but for the enemy and his fallen angels. The only humans that will go to hell are those who remain submitted to the enemy's authority and therefore part of his rebellion against God. A human's life is only meaningless when lived for itself apart from God. The meaning of life is found in this saying; "God so loved the world that he gave his only begotten Son and anyone who believes in him shall not perish but have everlasting life." Anyone who does not accept this saying is choosing hell on his own.

A man who walks off a cliff cannot accuse the bridge for being ignored. Jesus is the bridge over the chasm of sin and death and I stand now inviting you to cross. All who show the wisdom of crossing the bridge will be saved but all who follow the foolishness of walking off the cliff will fall into everlasting destruction."

The man from man fell back into the dust with much trembling.

Then the next man from man came forward and said: "I am living for free love. How can you condemn love of any kind? Any and all type of love is still love. How can you speak against me if God created me this way? Do you realize when you speak against me you are speaking against God who made me."

Then the prophet said: "You are deceived and taken captive to do evil against your own self. Yours is the most common reason for sin in the human heart for you say if I justify something in my own mind then it is acceptable to God. Do you not see that there is an eternal law that existed before the foundation of the world, and that your own reasons and justifications are of no consequence?

You speak of love but yours is not love but warped emotions. The enemy has caused a deep-seated hurt in your soul and uses this hurt to twist your emotions into expressing this lifestyle. From infancy the enemy has been hurting you and preparing you for this deception. Christ has died for you and loves you and has his hand extended to you to heal your emotions. This is true love. God is love so you cannot love anyone else outside of the law and love of God. You cannot express love through sin but through sin you will only express powerful twisted emotion.

You reject God's love and choose your emotions to justify your lifestyle. True love includes but is more than emotions. Emotions alone cannot lead you to love. Love flows through a relationship with God into us then out from us to the world around us. This is the only free love that exists for all other love is based on selfish emotion and has a cost attached. Understand there is no free love but God. God is free love.

You also claim that you are without guilt for you were created this way. The enemy works hurt and pain even in the womb, so from the beginning he has planted such deceptions in your heart. This deception started from your earliest memories and is associated with pain and rejection but you do not seek to be delivered from this deception or made whole, indeed you are seeking justification to continue in your wickedness. Your inclusion in the coming destruction is sure."

The man from man fell back into the dust with much weeping and gnashing of teeth.

The next man from man came forward and said: "I am a great Christian leader and I have seen that your views don't always agree with mine. What is the meaning of this?"

The prophet said: "The meaning of this is simple. You follow the doctrines of men. You draw nigh onto God with your mouth but your heart is far from him. God says the greatest of these is love but you won't give the poor a place among you in your pews, but only condescending charity and sometimes not even that. You look down on those who have been arrested and thrown in prison or are the rejected of our society.

God says love not the world, but you live according to every principal of the world. God says be Holy for I am Holy, but you practice all types of wickedness. You don't study God's Word or even know it but the traditions of your own denomination you take as truth. He who is not for Christ is against Christ he who does not gather with Christ scatters. Repent or you will be like the unwise virgins who had no oil and were left out in the darkness where there was weeping and gnashing of teeth."

The man from man fell back into the dust with much weeping and sorrow.

Then the last man from man came forward and said: "I am new age and I see that there are many truths. You shouldn't be so closed minded. Many sincere people are seeking help from spirit guides and others in the spirit world."

The prophet said to him: "Yes people are receiving from the spirit world but it is not help. They are receiving lies, deceptions and a gateway to eternal destruction as are you.
You say in your heart that everything that comes from the spirit world that feels helpful is good. You fail to recognize that there are powers, principalities and spiritual wickedness in high places who can transform themselves into angels of light. Even the enemy himself can appear to be an angel of light. These spirit deceivers give you sugar coated subtle deceptions and you receive them to your bosom.

Don't you know that in ancient Egypt the powers of darkness replicated many of the acts that God did through Moses? This is the spiritual reality you are receiving.

You call yourself 'New Age' but in reality, yours is wickedness of old. Indeed, the same lie that was told in Eden has been told to you by your spirit guides. The enemy told Eve that she would be like God and he tells you today that you are all God. Don't you know that from the beginning God forbade any spiritualist to be among his people? If you continue down this path you will share the drink of the cup of God's wrath with the rest of the lost."

The man from man fell back with much weeping and gnashing of teeth.

Then the Lord himself looked out from heaven to see all that goes on in the earth and the Lord said: "All creation is struggling with the berth pains of that great day and I perceive that the harvest is plentiful, but the workers are few. Who can I send to help with the harvest?"

Then the men from man came forward trembling with head bowed and while they were still afar off, they stopped and said: "Sovereign Lord, we now know you to be the only wise God and savior of the world. We know we are not worthy to come into your presence but we plead with you to count not our sin against others like us. Though we are destined to be lost send us to warn the world so they will not share in our destruction."

Then the Lord's heart was touched, and his love was manifested to the men from man and he said to them: "Men of God rise out of the dust. Come now and receive the white robes that were prepared for you before the foundation of the world."

Then the men from man that had been transformed into the men of God received their white robes, laying their former clothes aside and went forward throughout the earth proclaiming the good news of forgiveness for humanity and God's loving way to eternal life. And when the full measure of time had passed, they each went to their reward of eternal life and joy unspeakable and there they remained always along with all those who humble themselves before the knowledge of the Lord.

A Christian Reply To the reasonable Atheist...

...And A Message for the Thinking Christion Too

Introduction

One day a young African maiden from an important river village approached the village elders with a question. "We all know you are wise, and your guidance of our village is above reproach. What is the source of your mighty wisdom?"

The elders replied, "We get our wisdom from all around us; we are surrounded by it every day." The maiden then asked, "We know that you use this wisdom in giving names to all the new maidens born in our village. How does your wisdom know what to call us? How do you arrive at our names?"

The elders replied, "When we rise in the morning when the day is still new and the scent of the African violet permeates the air around us and a maiden is born, we name her 'Beautiful Flower.' Or when we rise in morning when the day is still new and the scent of the River Congo is in the air all around us and a maiden is born, we name her 'Fertile River.' But tell me 'Very Fresh Hippo Droppings,' why do you ask?"

This book seeks to change how the Christian faith is given its name among the atheist community.

Many atheists feel a deep, passionate, visceral rejection of the Christian faith, and a surprising number who do so were formerly Christians. Why would so many people, including a great many former Christians, reject the Chris- tian idea and take up atheism in a world where access to Christianity is everywhere? The explanation is simple, inoculation. Medical inoculation is "the exposure to a dead or weakened version of a virus to create a strong resistance to said virus." In our society, people have suffered a religious inoculation because of their exposure to dead and weak versions of Christianity. Dead or weak does not mean "inactive or limited," so this exposure is far-reaching and varied. From un-biblical fanaticism, like the burning of a Koran, to tepid pseudo-psychological preaching made available every day, people are constantly exposed to dead or weak versions of the Christian faith.

What makes these versions of Christianity dead or weak is not a lack of fervor or commitment; these versions seem to have no shortage of that. Instead these versions lack an authentic ministry of God's Word in the experience. A Christian faith without a vibrant, consistent, and credible Bible foundation is not a Christian faith at all. Considering this, I am fearful that many atheists have developed their passionate resistance to all things Christian- based on something other than a living, Biblical Christian faith. Most atheists have questions that can easily be answered for them from an authentic Christian perspective.

In A Christian Reply to the Reasonable Atheist, an authentic Christian narrative will be explored, using the first three chapters of Genesis as a launching point. The question of evil, Hell, the origin of religion, and more will be explored as this treatise seeks to change how the Christian church is named among atheist. This book is not a theological treatment of the Bible; there is no shortage of such books. Rather, this book is designed as a Biblical framing of an authentic personal faith—a framing that will convey the Biblical heart of Christian beliefs in a personal, intimate way.

It is my prayer and belief that many of my Christian brothers and sisters will benefit from the Biblical explanations contained within the pages. This book, however, is not designed as a Christian self-help book; there is no shortage of those books either. This book is designed to provide an alternative to religious inoculation to any reasonable person, but more than all, it is intended as a Chris- tian reply to the rational, reasonable atheist.

–Vernon L. Harper 2013

Chapter 1 Instructions and the Tech Manual

The Judeo-Christian Big Bang, Genesis

"Understanding is the reward of faith. Therefore, seek not to understand that you may believe, but believe that you may understand."

St. Augustine

Large parts of the nature of the universe have been explained simply because of one assumption: The Big Bang. When science observed that the universe was expanding, it immediately begged an answer to the question, "From what?" The idea that the universe had a beginning and was not static and eternal was completely revolutionary. This idea allowed science to play fill in the blanks with the notions that the Big Bang suggest.

Many of the cosmological discoveries of the last 60 years were a result of the scientists' acceptance of the Big Bang theory and allowing that idea to form the basis for what they observed about the universe. As a result of this assumption, computer models were created, mathematical equations were computed, and laboratory experiments were conducted, all to fill in the framework of the ideas created by the Big Bang. The Big Bang did not answer every question but became a type of template or guide- line for what scientists should expect to see, and a clearer picture of the universe resulted.

The Judeo-Christian tradition has a similar template or guideline—the first three chapters of the book of Genesis. The first three chapters of Genesis do for the history of man and the truth of the Bible what the Big Bang does for our understanding of the universe. If we assume these chapters in Genesis to be true, it informs all that we see in human history and Scripture. Like the template of the Big Bang, the template of the first three chapters of Genesis does not immediately answer every question; however, these chapters do provide us with a direction of inquiry and a guideline for what we should expect to see.

This template, however, cannot be accessed if you dis- miss the Bible and the book of Genesis as just another book of religious myths and stories. The Bible is not sim- ply a book but the revelation of God to His creation.

I would ask you to accept, just for the sake of argument and the length of this book, the faith-based assumption that God exists and that He is revealed through the Bible. It is only in this way that we can begin to examine the Christian narrative through accessing the Bible's true wealth and depth.

If we accept that God has created the heavens and the earth and expressed His nature and the nature of His creation through the Bible, should we then expect the Bible to be any less vast, nuanced and layered than the universe? The reason that we can fail to realize the true nature of the Bible is simply a matter of perception. Faith-based Perception Vs. Material-based Perception.

When our intellect receives its decision-making information from the material world, our perspective can be called material perception. When our intellect receives its decision-making information from other than the material world, our perspective can be called one of faith. Mate- rial perception leads our intellect to reason. When faith
is directed toward God, then that faith leads our intellect toward revelation.

Revelation is "the God-given perception of realities and truths that exist outside of material perception."

Trying to perceive faith-based revelation through mate- rial-based reason is impossible because the organ of perception for each is of two different natures. The organ of perception for revelation is faith directed toward God, but the organ of perception for reason is material perception. Trying to perceive revelation through material perception is the equivalent of trying to perceive color through your ear.

This is the main reason why the wealth of the Bible is not perceived by many intellectuals who make the mis- take of approaching the Bible strictly by material perception. Revelation is the only way the Bible (or God, for that matter) can be perceived. Yes, there is reasoned Biblical scholarship, but the foundation for that Biblical scholar- ship is Biblical revelation. For the Christian scholar, rea- son is the tool of faith-based revelation.

There is no way to enter into a serious discussion of the Christian idea outside of the context of the Bible, and it is impossible to examine the Bible from any other perspective except one of revelation through faith.

Revelation reveals mysteries, and mysteries remain mysteries and can always only be accessed through rev- elation. If a person comes to receive understanding of a mystery through revelation and then tries to explain this mystery to others, those others will not understand just because they are told. Those others will also have to access the perception of the mystery on their own through revelation. This is the ministry of God's Word—providing truth to humanity to be rejected by reason or embraced by revelation.

The door to revelation is simply faith, believing God. It has to be this way. If God revealed Himself through our intellect, all of us would fail to know God. God is so far above and beyond human ability to comprehend or understand Him through reason that the only way any- one can know Him is through revelation. Revelation also levels the playing field. Access to God should not be measured out to humanity based on individual intelligence. Through revelation, everyone has equal access to the living God.

Revelation cannot be conveyed through reason because revelation explained is like a joke explained. You can be given all the appropriate information, but reason will not produce the desired effect of the joke or of revelation. This is why arguing the validity of the Bible is useless. It is impossible to argue revelation.

There are times when someone, through material perception, will pick a point of contention in the Bible and attack it in an effort to disprove the Bible's validity. This ploy is equivalent to picking up an unsolved question about the universe and using it to prove that the Big Bang is false. The Bible must be accepted as the revelation of God. Only then can a person begin to solve its individual mysteries through revelation.

For our purposes here, let us assume, for at least the length of this book and for the sake of argument, that the Genesis template is true. In this way we can access the Christian concept of revelation-based knowledge and use it to begin to examine how the Bible addresses the human condition.

Now that we have established how the Christian narrative should be approached, let's dive headlong into Genesis.

The Tech Manual

In the first chapter of Genesis, we are given how the heavens and the earth were made. Chapter 1 of Genesis is like a manufacturer's technical manual. Chapter 1 tells us how everything was made and reveals to us aspects of the function and nature of what was made in a linear nuts and bolts kind of way.

In this first chapter, we see that everything was made by God's speaking it into existence in six separate periods of the expression of God's will. We tend to define these periods or days as some length of time, and this definition is quite possibly true. However, the most important concept to grasp is that these six separate days represent six separate periods of God's light or expressions of God's will.

There are those who point to the fossil record and mistakenly say that it contradicts the Creation history in Genesis. The fossil record does not disagree with God's creating life within periods of the expression of light. This mistaken assumption can only be made by a misreading of Genesis.

When in verse 2 of the first chapter of Genesis, God says, "Let there be light," He is likely speaking of physical light, but He is certainly speaking of spiritual light, which is the expression of His will in Creation. The days or periods that follow are separate periods of light or expressions of the will of God. This idea is mirrored in the Gospel of John in verses 1 through 5. John tells us how everything was made through the Word of God, and in that Word of God was life, and this life is the light of humanity. Suffice it to say that the light as the expression of God's will in Creation is a theme that runs throughout the entire Bible and is foundational to the Christian faith. The periods of light (or days) in Genesis are periods of the expression of God's will in Creation.

The fact that everything else was made first then humanity was introduced after all of Creation had been prepared and that humanity was given dominion over it, all implies that Creation was all prepared for humans. The purpose of all the furnishings of Genesis chapter 1 was to prepare the earth for humanity.

In this tech manual, we are also given something of the nature and purpose of humanity. In verses 26 through 28 of chapter 1, we are told that God created humanity male and female. God does not make any distinctions between the nature and purpose of man and women because there are none. Humanity as manifested in male and female form is given dominion over the earth and every living thing on it. Who was created first, who first heard God's commandment, and everything detailed later is not relevant to the tech manual. There is no human and vice- human in God's Creation. The man and the woman are two equal parts of humanity in its entirety; if you subtract one, you no longer have humanity as created by God. This idea is echoed in Genesis 5:1-2. The equality of man and woman was our original state.

Humanity—man and woman—is made in the image and likeness of God. This does not mean that as I write this text that God could use our hair products or copy our daily workout regimes. God is a Spirit and expresses His will as light throughout the universe and beyond. Humanity being created in the image and likeness of God means that humanity was originally created as a spiritual being that can express its will as God's light in the mate- rial world. It is the spirit in humanity that results in the image and likeness of God, and this image and likeness or light found its unique expression through the exercising of dominion on the earth.

In verses 26 through 28 of chapter 1, God says He will make humanity in His image and likeness and continues in the same thought to describe the expression of this likeness by declaring the dominion of humanity over the earth. As spiritual souls, we were uniquely able to be God's representatives in the earth—His bearers of light. We were hardwired with the image and likeness or light of God to exercise dominion over the earth, and as we were in relationship and subject to the Spirit of God, the earth would become in relationship and subject to God through us.

This idea implies that the earth was not completely in agreement or subject to God for why else would humanity have to fill the earth and subdue it? For man to dominate the earth and bring it under subjection means it wasn't under subjection already.

I will pause here at the precipice of a theological cliff that I refuse to jump off. Between Genesis 1:1 and 1:2 is a chasm of theological debate. Some scholars will say that verse 2 indicates Creation incomplete, and what follows is God's completing His Creation. Others say that verse 2 indicates Creation after some cataclysmic event, namely the fall of Lucifer, and what follows is God's giving order to the chaos caused by this cataclysm. I ascribe to the latter, and the only defense I will give of this belief is what is contained in the rest of this work. I would refer you to the many theological works, of which this is not one, to answer your potential questions. I believe that the rest of Scripture, especially Genesis chapters 1 through 3, agrees with this view. I also believe this view gives us a good explanation for the age of the earth. We are also not told if there were animals in the Creation before this cataclysm, but if so, it is one of several explanations for the age of life on earth. I only mention these views here because they are sure to put some theologian's nose out of joint, so I wanted to acknowledge the opinion and stance I am taking.

Humanity's original nature was to express the nature of God and to bring the earth back under the subjection of God in every way. Humanity was created with innate ability and was armed with every authority to accomplish the task of subduing the earth. We were to be God's representatives in the earth and to enjoy close personal relationship with Him.

Well, what happened?

Chapter 2 A Play Entitled "What Happened"

Act 1

If chapter 1 of Genesis is the tech manual, chapters 2 and 3 can be described as an emotional and tragic play portraying love in its highest form, damaged relationships, betrayed intimacy, redemption, and mercy.

Setting the Stage and Introducing the Main Characters

The following is a list of those whom I would cast for a current production:

God. . . . . .played by Himself
Adam. . . . . .played by Every Man
Eve. . . . . played by Every Woman
The Devil. . . . . .played by the Serpent
The Tree of the
Knowledge of
Good and Evil. . . . . . .played by Rad Daly (He played the apple from the Fruit of the Loom commercials.)

In Act 1 the cast of characters will be established, the scene will be set to portray the relationships of Genesis, chapter 2. Then we will explore the story of this tragic play in Acts 2 and 3 found in Genesis, chapter 3.

In Genesis 2:7 we are given the nature of God's relationship with us through the details of humanity's creation. It is a very intimate and personal scene with God's taking inert material, carefully, lovingly and intricately forming us and then breathing out of His own Being the breath or spirit of life, and we became a living soul. We were essentially a lovingly crafted soul made alive by God's Spirit.

This close personal relationship cannot be overstated. God breathed out of Himself and gave us part of Who He is, and humanity became forever bearers of His image and likeness. It is a relationship closer than any father and child. God loves humanity with a pure, sacrificial, and protective love. God loves mankind with a parental love untarnished by selfish expectations, human frailty, or misguided action. The love of the God of the universe has its ultimate ex- pression as His breathing of spiritual life out of His innermost being into His unique creation—humanity. This spirit in us allows us to be aware of and have a relationship with the living spiritual God. It is because of this spirit or breath that we could be described as a living soul. Our spirit through our soul expressed the life of the living God. God created humanity in three parts: spirit, soul, and body. This threefold nature distinguishes humanity from the animals that God created. In verse 19 of this second chapter, in a similar fashion to the way He created humanity, God created the animals from the ground. However, God did not breathe into them the breath of life. Yes, they are biologically alive, but they did not receive God's image and likeness. Our body and soul, or flesh, was fashioned from the ground, but we were made spiritually alive from the breath of God.

The body is how humanity experiences the material world, and the soul is how humanity processes, responds to, and expresses itself in the material world. In the Bible the body and soul together are referred to as the flesh, and the flesh is the organ of interaction with the material world. The spirit is how humanity carried and expressed the image and likeness of God. The spirit and soul are distinct and of two different natures.

The following two Scriptures support the distinction between spirit and soul and the threefold nature of man.

Hebrews 4:12, "For the word of God is living and active, sharper than any two-edged sword, piercing the division of soul and spirit...."

1 Thessalonians 5:23, "May the God of peace himself sanctify you wholly; and may your spirit, soul and body be kept sound and blameless at the coming of our Lord Jesus Christ."

Our spirit allows us to operate in the spiritual realm. Our spirit operates in communion, conscience, and intuition.

Communion is how spiritual humanity relates with a spiritual God. God is Spirit, and He can only be reached spiritually. It is our spirit that gave us the ability to do so.

Conscience is how the image and likeness of God is expressed to the soul. What made our soul a living soul was our conscience leading us every second that we lived to express the image and likeness of God.

Intuition is how our spirit reveals to us what is true in the material world and the spiritual realm. Revelation is given through our spiritual intuition.

The following are some Scriptures which demonstrate that our spirits move in communion, conscience and intuition.

Communion

John 4:23, "The true worshippers will worship the father in spirit and in truth."
Luke 1:47, "My spirit rejoices in God my savior."

Conscience

Proverbs 20:27, "The spirit in man is the lamp of the Lord, Searching all the inner depths of his heart."
Acts 17:16, "His spirit was provoked within him as he saw the city full of Idols."

Intuition

Ephesians 1:17, "...that the God of our Lord Jesus Christ the father of glory may give you the spirit of wisdom and revelation in the knowledge of him,"
Matthew 16:17, "...for flesh and blood did not reveal this to you, but My father who is in heaven."

The soul as the individual expression of humanity, is where our personhood—our individual personality—resides. The soul is made up of our will, intellect, and emotion. The following Scriptures demonstrates that the soul moves in will, intellect, and emotions.

Will

Psalm 62:1, "Truly my soul silently waits for God; from him comes my salvation."
Psalm 34:2, "My soul shall make its boast in the Lord; the humble shall hear of it and be glad."

Intellect

Psalm 139:14b, "...Marvelous are your works, And that my soul knows very well."
Proverbs 19:2a, "Also it is not good that a soul be without knowledge...."

Emotion

Psalm 35:9, "And my soul shall be joyful in the Lord; It shall rejoice in His salvation."
John 12:27a, "Now my soul is troubled...."

The body is the means of how we function in the material world. The body's general functions include appetite, self-preservation, and procreation. Our body's function in appetite not only in the obvious food and drink but also in temperature, rest sunlight, and anything that is necessary for biological survival.

The reason why a person cannot commit suicide by holding his breath is that the body functions in self-preservation—separate and distinct from the human soul. The body does its best to fight off infections, repair itself, respond to trauma, and adapt to changing environments, etc. The body performs these functions and others apart from the will, intellect, and emotion of the soul.

The body also functions in reproduction. The healthy body is constantly ready to reproduce, and unless precautions are taken will reproduce in a sexually active person quite apart from their will, intellect, or emotion.

In his book, *The Spiritual Man*, the Christian teacher, and writer, Watchman Nee likened the function of humanity's threefold nature to a light bulb. The invisible power of the bulb is the electricity, and the invisible power behind man's unique nature is the spirit. The invisible power of the bulb is expressed as visible light, and our invisible spirit was expressed through the will, intellect, and emotions of the soul. The glass, the filament and other parts of the bulb are equivalent to our physical body. The bulb (body) is filled with the power (spirit) and expresses the light (soul). Humanity—man and woman—truly functioned as a living soul. The God-given spirit was expressed as a soul contained in a body. This is how the spirit of humanity; the image and likeness of God was expressed in the material world. We expressed light as God's unique representative in the earth.

The way humanity, Adam, and Eve functioned was spirit-led. When it was time to nourish the body, the spirit through the conscious function of the spirit expressed to the soul that it was time to nourish the body. The soul's intellect directed the particulars of the how, the where, and the what of acquiring food. The emotions of the soul felt the thankfulness to God for the garden and the food as well as the joy of tasting and sharing the food. The will said, "Let's do it," and the body carried out the direction of the will, and the body was nourished.

I am stating these functions as separate parts of the one action of nourishing the body for clarity of the nature of each function, but the reality was that they were seam- less and moved as one function as electricity is expressed as light from a light bulb. This was the original nature of humanity.

In addition to humanity, there are three distinct types of entities each with their own natures.

1) God caused plant life to spring out of the ground as biological life only (Genesis 2:9). Their expression in the material Creation is limited to their biological functions. Plants can adapt and respond to their environment, ingest nutrition in an attempt to fight off disease, and reproduce themselves, but they can do nothing beyond body function. Plant life does not have souls; therefore, the plant life cannot move in will, intellect, and emotion.

2) Animal life was crafted from the ground by God in a similar fashion to humanity with a soul and a body. The Biblical designation for soul and body is the flesh. Animals can move in

will, intellect, and emotion as they respond to and express themselves in the material world. Animals, however, do not have a spirit. God did not breathe into them His spirit. They cannot move in the spiritual, and therefore lack all the higher creativity, ambition, and enlightenment of humanity.

3) We must take some time to introduce this last entity that exists. Some of you will no doubt think I have entered the realm of the impossible, but Scripture has much to teach of the ministering spirits called angels.

Angels are described in Scripture as "ministering spirits" and are spirit only. Angels can express the will of God in the material world and seem only under the authority of God to be able to take physical form. Angels do not have souls or bodies. Angels predate the creativity of God that started in the second verse of chapter one of Genesis. They predate and are not included in the Creation information of the tech manual.

There is also a category of angels in Scripture that can be described as fallen. These angels have rebelled against God and live to express their will in the material world. We
should note that the only angels that we find in Scripture that take physical form are those operating under the ex- press authority and will of God. Fallen angels always only seem to be acting through the manipulation of humanity and human authority.

Before you reject the notion of spiritual beings called angels, I would ask you to humor me and assume that the template of Genesis is true until this framing of a personal faith is completed and context has been provided for the given information.

The Love Interest

God created humanity in two equal, but distinct, parts— male and female. There is no "vice-human" or one part of humanity that was created to be subservient or inferior to the other. The tech manual of the first chapter of Genesis reveals this fact. The second chapter of Genesis shows the specific and distinct roles of man and woman and the nature of their relationship.

Allow me to pause here to attempt to understand the original nature of humanity. The man and woman in the Garden were in every way superior to humanity today. We can hardly imagine the original nature of humanity. To ex- press the living God without fail in every aspect of your life is something we cannot comprehend—not just in the negative aspect of not violating that nature by choosing other than God's will but the positive aspect of always ex- pressing yourself as God's light.

The man and woman completely expressing the image and likeness of God had ramifications for the material world. To be the image of God is to be representative of the light of God with every expression of your being in the material world. The likeness of God is to influence, to affect change in, and to exercise dominion over the mate- rial world through the light of God. This state of being is almost impossible for us to fathom.

Can you imagine never eating a half teaspoon more or less of food than is necessary to nourish the body? Can you imagine not resting a half a second more or less than is re- quired for the body? Can you imagine having the dominion over everything in the entire world? Every plant, animal, the sea, the rivers the mountains, everything in the mate- rial world was subject to you. Can you imagine having the power to subdue the entire material world, having the ability to see beyond what the material world shows you, and having the knowledge of how to interact with everything in the material world through spiritual revelation? These things I mention are just scratching the surface of humanity's original nature. We get a hint of this nature when we see Jesus, the second Adam, exercising His authority in the material world, but I am getting ahead of myself. Suffice it to say that humanity—man and woman—in the Garden were of a completely superior nature and had completely superior abilities than we can fully know or comprehend.

In Genesis 2:15, the first thing we are told about the role of the man is that God put the man in the Garden of Eden to tend and keep it. The man's job was not only to tend ("cultivate") but also to keep ("protect"). This word definition begs an answer to the question, "Protect it from what?" What was outside of the will of God that required the keeping of the Garden against it? This question will be
addressed a little later, but for now, let's just acknowledge that the man's role included protecting the Garden and everything in it.

Directly after the man was given the role to tend and protect the Garden in Genesis 2:15, he is given in verse 17 the only command that God gives in the Garden. That command was not to eat from the tree of the knowledge of good and evil.

It is interesting to note that God did not give the man a command to tend and keep the Garden or have dominion over the earth. Placing the man in the Garden with God's image and likeness was enough, and the man would naturally express himself in the tending and keeping of the garden and the subduing of the rest of the world.

God gave the man this command because of Genesis 1:29. In this Scripture, God had given humanity every plant for food. In addition to this gift, it was in man's nature to be curious and have dominion over everything in the earth. This tree would have been no exception.

Right after God gave him the commandment, God states that it is not good for the man to be alone and that He would make a comparable help meet for him. God creates and brings the various animals to the man to see what he would call them in verse 19. God is giving the man his first act of dominion by allowing him to decide the animal's names. God Himself seems excited as He watched to see what His beloved humanity would name the animals.

In Scripture, names are significant; they usually rep- resented something of the nature of the thing or person named. God gave the man the name Adam because that name is associated with the earth, and Adam would forever
be associated with the earth with which he was created. Adam named his wife Eve because Eve means "to live," and she would forever be the mother of all the living. The man's assigning the names of the animals is significant be- cause the man is not just arbitrarily throwing names at the animals but is discerning and even perhaps helping to craft their natures with the names he is giving them. In verse 20 the man had discerned the nature of every animal and declared by what names they would be known, but among them no comparable helper was found for him.

What happens next in verses 21 through 25 is the start of the greatest romantic tragedy in human history. God caused Adam to fall into a deep sleep, and during that deep sleep, He took part of Adam's flesh—his rib—and crafted the Woman. God did not start from scratch and create an entirely new human. God took part of humanity already created and formed the woman. The man and woman were of the same flesh. There can be no more intimate relationship than this. They were functioning as one body and soul. Yes, the woman had a separate body as well as a separate soul, but the man and the woman functioned as one flesh—which is one body and soul. They were a united front as they functioned in Creation. The man and woman did not love each other like they loved their own body and soul, but in their hearts, they were one flesh. No separation or disparity could exist, so they loved and cared for each other as they loved and cared for themselves. When the man, in verse 23, says, "This is now bone of my bone and flesh of my flesh," he is pronouncing the most intimate of possible relationships—oneness of flesh.

The man then makes the proclamation of what the nature of all future marriages could have been in verse 24, which says, "Therefore a man shall leave his father and mother and be joined to his wife and the two shall become one flesh." Adam's declaration provides humanity with an insight into his original powers for he is displaying fore- sight and wisdom of a high order. Adam immediately comprehends the significance of his relationship with Eve, and he also understands the significance of this relationship for all yet unborn humanity. To understand and foresee this future state in the first moment of seeing Eve shows a power, a mastery, and an understanding of his circum- stance beyond anything humanity can now exercise.

Verse 25 shares that the man and woman were naked and not ashamed. I know what some of you might be thinking, but I can assure you their lack of shame was not a function of their winter diet or workout regime. But I must say if believing that in some small measure will motivate you to work out and eat right, what could it hurt? You can call it "The Eden Before the Fall Diet and Workout Plan." The plan would consist of working in a garden and eating vegetables. That plan certainly wouldn't be any more ridiculous than many of the diet and workout plans already on the market, but I digress. Where was I? Oh yes, the man and the woman were naked and not ashamed.

Humanity—the man and the woman—in Eden ex- pressed only the light of God in their every motive, thought and action and had no knowledge of anything outside of God's light. They lived and moved and had their being only in the spirit given them by God when humanity was fashioned. Shame derives from the knowledge of a personal motive, thought or action that is outside of the light of God. Shame and the accompanying fear were not possible for beings whose

life entire flowed completely from the light of God and was not dependent on choosing from their own "soulish" knowledge of good and evil.

Act 2

The Introduction of the Remainder of the Cast

So far in this tragic play, God, the Man and the Woman have been introduced. Now the final two characters must be presented: the tree of the knowledge of good and evil and the Serpent.

The tree of the knowledge of good and evil represented a fundamental change in the nature of humanity. For humanity to partake of that tree was to change from a being that expressed the light of God from their spirit's conscious outward in every motive, thought and action to a being that expressed the results of its own material perception that was based on the knowledge of what it perceived as good and what it perceived as evil. Once the fundamental nature of humanity became one of material perception of the soul and increasingly excluding humanity's spirit which was made in the image and likeness of God, then all humanity was doomed to increasingly make choices contrary to the light of God and humanity's conscience was relegated to a still, small voice that was summarily ignored. Originally humanity—man and woman—was led by the light of God. That light from their spirit led them in when,

how and to what degree to nourish their bodies, but after partaking of "the tree of the knowledge of good and evil" their will, intellect and emotions determined when, how and to what degree to nourish themselves. Every time they nourished their bodies, it was done just a little more contrary to the light of God. One teaspoon too much would become one tablespoon too much and thirty seconds too early became one minute to early because it was based on their own will, intellect, and emotions, which is the mate- rial perception of the soul. The nature of "the tree of the knowledge of good and evil" was to increasingly lead humanity away from the light of God and into the darkness of humanity's own soul-based choices.

We are told in Genesis that the Serpent was more cunning than any beast of the field that the Lord God had made. This fact is important to show why it was the ser- pent and not one of the other animals that had deceived humanity. What it does not tell us is why would any of the animals, including the serpent, be motivated to cause humanity to disobey God? How would any of the animals understand the consequences for humanity enough to move in such a way to bring about the exact action that would cause the Fall?

For the answer to these questions, Genesis 1:1-2 must be consulted. In the first chapter of Genesis, God created the heavens and the earth. In the second verse of Genesis, the earth was void and without form. The question is "What could have happened that could have transformed God's Creation into a place that is void and without form? The answer is the fallen angel, Lucifer. In the fourteenth chapter of the book of Isaiah and beginning in the twelfth verse, a detailed description of the fall of the angel Lucifer is prophetically given. This fallen angel's desire was to op- pose and usurp the will of God in any possible way.

If it is true that the age of life on earth is explained by God's original Creation that existed before verse 2 of Genesis, then it is possible for Lucifer to have expressed himself through that life and caused the cataclysm that occurred between verse 1 and verse 2 of the first chapter of Genesis. I am not attempting to establish to a theological certainty that this is what happened; rather, my desire is but only to show the possibility for this fall to have occurred. Certainly, Scripture does not prohibit this idea for the fall of Lucifer. I only mention this possibility to give those who disagree with this premise the foundation of my idea for their own inquiry and study.

Angels are not mentioned in the tech manual beginning in Genesis 1:2 because they predate verse two. Also, the fallen angels mentioned in Scripture fell before verse 2. Lucifer's and his angels' fall led to the corruption of God's original Creation. The fallen angel Lucifer was in the world and opposed to God's light at the time that humanity was in Eden, and angels are spirit only and cannot express themselves in the material world. To express themselves in the material world, a fallen angel would need a soul comprised of will, intellect and emotion. For Lucifer to express himself in the material world, it would make perfect sense for him to use the abilities of the most cunning creature to orchestrate the Fall of humanity. Lucifer is not mentioned by name in Eden, but he is present and expressing himself through the soul of the serpent.

In the twenty-eighth chapter starting at the eleventh verse of the Biblical book of Ezekiel, a detailed description of the fallen angel called Lucifer is given. In verses 1 through 10, God's pronouncement of judgment on the wicked prince of Tyre is given.

Starting at verse 11, God's description and pronouncing of judgment on the power behind the wicked prince of Tyre called the King of Tyre is given. This power was Lucifer. Ezekiel 28:13 says this king behind the prince of Tyre was in Eden. The beginning of a detailed description of this king's unusual appearance is given.

Lucifer had previously caused the corruption of God's Creation between verse 1 and verse 2 of the first chapter of the book of Genesis. It is true we are not told specifically how the previous world was corrupted or if life existed and if it did exist, how it was corrupted. We do know, however, that Lucifer was in Eden, and that he had motive and opportunity to corrupt the reorganized world through humanity, who had been given the charge, the authority, and the ability to subdue and protect this reorganized world for God.

A Cunning Plan

Lucifer's expressing himself through the soul of the serpent was able to get humanity to surrender the image and likeness of God expressed in the human spirit and to rely completely on the perception of the human soul. His plan succeeded because of his understanding of the nature of humanity and the nature and vulnerabilities of the relationship between the man and the woman. As previously mentioned, the man and the woman were equal parts of humanity that fulfilled two distinct roles. Eve was created to be the help meet of Adam but not the servant. Get rid of all the notions of barefoot and pregnant or slaving over a hot stove while the man went out to work and returned in time to watch Monday night football and smoke fat cigars. That description is fallen humanity's notion of Eve's role in Eden.

In Eden Eve was a help meet—not a vice-human. She was half

of humanity and took care of everything pertaining to Adam's role in the world while Adam cared for the Garden to expand and protect it. Adam also lovingly cared for and protected everything that pertained to Eve. They had different roles in the dominion and subduing of the earth and different roles in relation toward each other, and yet they were equals.

It would be difficult to give too much attention to the nature of Adam and Eve's relationship. This relationship that should have been forever the standard for all future marriages is difficult to comprehend. Can we really know what it is like to be half of a whole and to have that whole expressed as God's light? Can we likewise know what it is like not to love each other but to love the entity that is both of you—one flesh—completely and without restraint. This was the nature of their relationship. This is what we must strive to understand if we are to begin to comprehend what was lost in the Fall and the nature of the deception that caused that Fall.

Eve took care of everything that pertained to Adam. Eve lovingly deciding when and how Adam should be nourished would not be unusual, and Adam's lovingly accepting this watch care would also not be unusual.

In verse 1 of chapter 3 of Genesis when Lucifer, through the serpent, poses a question to Eve, that question is pregnant with the notion of Eve's deciding what was good for Adam. Eve's role of wanting what was good for her Adam would have stimulated her to consider anything that could be a benefit. In asking if God really said that they could not partake of every tree from the Garden, the serpent is causing her to apply her own powers of reason to God's commandment and to what was best for everything pertaining to her and her Adam.

We know Eve is relying on her own intellect and not the commandment itself to deal with the question posed by the serpent because in her answer she is trying to make God's commandment more reasonable. Eve does so by adding to God's commandment by saying in verse 3 that they could not even touch the fruit from the tree, or they would die. God never said anything about not touching the tree.

At this point Eve is doomed to fall because now God's Word was not enough for her; she had to justify it by the standard of her own intellect. She stated that the fruit was so deadly it could not even be touched. Eve is using her material perception to examine and to explain the reason for God's command. "Of course, we can't eat from this tree; God is protecting us from this horribly deadly fruit." The serpent can now show her by her own material perception that the tree is not deadly—at least not in a way she could comprehend. The serpent goes on to suggest that the fruit of this tree will actually provide a benefit, and that not only is God jealously withholding this benefit from her, but more importantly from her Adam. The serpent tells Eve in verses 4 and 5 that she and her Adam will not die, and that God's real motive for the command was not to protect them but to keep them from becoming like God. How ironic that the very thing God sought to have humanity exist as—beings in His image and likeness—the serpent told Eve God was trying to prohibit.

In verse 6 Eve saw (material perception) that the fruit from this tree was good for food, pleasant to the eye, and good to make one wise. She then ate the fruit and gave it to her Adam with her. Eve was deceived about God's motives for forbidding the fruit from the tree of the knowledge of good and evil, but she was also deceived about Adam's ability to know and provide what was good for them. Eve received God's word from Adam because God spoke this commandment to Adam in Genesis 2:17 before Eve had been created. Eve received the word of God from Adam, so to doubt that word was to doubt her Adam. Eve had to conclude that Adam had failed to provide for them the truth and protect them from a lie. This failure of Eve to trust her Adam in the matter of God's word became the root of all such failures to trust in all future relationships.

Eve ate from the tree because she was deceived by the serpent through her material perception, but Adam was not deceived. Adam heard the command directly from God. This original sin is called the sin of Adam because he chose to receive from Eve's hand instead of obeying God's command. His Eve offered him to partake of the fruit, and he did partake in direct disobedience to the Word that God spoke to him.

The human soul is made up of will, intellect and emotion. The serpent accessed the soul of Eve through her intellect and reason but accessed the soul of Adam through his emotion and love.

Every act between Adam and Eve before the Fall was an act of intimate love and secure relationship unpolluted by fallen motives. Eve's deciding and providing what Adam ate was an act of pure love and intimacy, and Adam's receiving from his Eve's loving hand was also a pure and loving act. Eve was deceived through the twisting of her intellect by material perception, but Adam was seduced by the twisting of his emotion through that same material perception. Adam partook of the tree of the knowledge of good and evil not because he was deceived but because he chose the loving and intimate act of his Eve providing what she thought was a benefit to him over the revealed Word of God.

Overriding God's will with our own will is still the source of all human failure. Following material perception through our emotions or our intellect and ignoring the revealed will of God as expressed by the given Word of God is still how humanity is daily alienated from the living God.

Adam's sin was essentially the selfish act of partaking of Eve's intimacy and love instead of protecting her from the deception and obeying God's express command. This act of Adam's became the root of all future betrayal of intimacy in relationships as well as the first act of selfishly choosing to partake of a woman's intimacy instead of protecting her. Adam's love for his Eve was twisted into a weapon that was used against humanity's relationship with God and ironically a weapon against Eve through the Fall.

The Fall In

The act of Adam and Eve's partaking of the fruit of the tree of the knowledge of good and evil changed humanity forever. Humanity was created to procreate—to bring forth offspring in its image and likeness. Just as God created Adam and Eve in His image and likeness, He created humanity with the ability to procreate in its image and like- ness. Not only do children inherit physical characteristics from their parents, but they inherit the spiritual characteristics of their parents.

When Adam and Eve fell into sin by the changing of their essential nature from creatures that expressed the light of the living God to creatures that expressed the darkness of their own arbitrary knowledge of what was good and what was evil, all of their offspring fell with them. Every human born after the Fall was born in the image and like- ness of fallen parents.

The human condition became very different after the Fall. In verse 7 of the third chapter of Genesis, Adam and Eve's eyes were open, and immediately Adam and Eve suddenly knew what shame was. Shame derives from "the knowledge of a thought, motive or action that is outside of the light of God."

For creatures of light to suddenly fall into expressing darkness and to know what they had become and to understand why they had become it would be extremely traumatic. To feel shame, fear and mistrust for the first time after living with total security, authority, love, and do- minion would be confusing, frightening, disorienting and painful. When Adam and Eve's eyes were opened and they discovered the knowledge of what was good and what was evil, they could no longer trust their own or each other's thoughts, motives and actions. This knowledge ungoverned by God's light and only restrained by their soulish choices produced shame.

This is the beginning of the necessity for human law. Adam and Eve, because of their knowledge of what was good and evil, took fig leaves and covered themselves. God did not give Adam and Eve a command to cover them- selves because they ate of the tree. Humanity themselves created this law of being covered because of their knowledge of good and evil. When evil motives, thoughts and actions became available, humanity immediately became creatures that could only live by laws. When there is the knowledge of evil, then there is also the potential for evil. This potential for evil necessitates laws in an attempt to curb that evil. Human law was necessary because of the Fall, but human law was inadequate. Law could not curb the human condition of falling increasingly into evil. Hu- man law would only make that evil known by addressing it before all. Human law is also an attempt to quarantine evil to the motives and thoughts of the human heart and prevent it from spreading into human actions. One needs only to read a history book to see the failure of human law's ability to curb the darkness of human action.

I will pause here to speak to those people—including a great many Christians who think that law or religious dogma were God's idea for curing humanity and making humanity acceptable to him. God gave humanity just one law—the commandment not to eat from the tree of the knowledge of good and evil. The purpose of that commandment was not to curb the darkness of human action because human darkness did not yet exist; however, the purpose of that one law was to protect humanity from the Fall and death. This law was an expression of a loving relationship.

Human law, on the other hand, was a human invention to attempt to cover the human shame of our thoughts and motives, curb the human expression of darkness through our actions, and give us a false sense of righteousness. There is no law or religious dogma that can cure humanity or restrain its wicked actions. These wicked actions are just expressions of wicked thoughts and motives, and hu- man laws and religious dogmas have no power over human thoughts and motives.

All God-given law, including the Ten Commandments, were not given as a cure for human wickedness, but was a way for God to intercede in a system of laws that man had already begun. Man's inability to keep the law of God exposed the hopelessness of man's condition and his need for a cure. God did not give man His law primarily because of the actions it produced in humanity because humanity always failed to keep these laws anyway. God gave us His law because His law would give man the opportunity to turn his thoughts and motives toward the desire to please God.

All the dietary and the other Mosaic laws that God gave Israel were not an end in of itself but were primarily designed to turn Israel's thoughts and motives toward pleasing God and away from a self-centered knowledge of good and evil. When Israel kept the law, they were setting themselves apart as a people whose thoughts and motives

were turned to attempting to do the will of God. Keeping the law could not make Israel more righteous than the rest of humanity nor did the law have the power to change every human thought and motive. The law only gave Israel the opportunity to express through their actions the desire to make the will of God superior to their own notions of what was good and what is evil.

Are our thoughts and motives, as expressed by our actions, turned toward expressing the light of the living God Who lovingly breathed life into humanity in Eden? This is the crucial question. This is the only value of laws and religious dogmas.

Act 3

The Wheels on the Bus Go Round and Round...

In Genesis 3:8, the damage caused to the relationship of God and His beloved humanity is realized. Where love, trust and fellowship once flourished now there is mistrust, fear, and alienation. Humanity hid from the Living God without provocation. Can you imagine a parent's coming home from work to children who they have loved and cared for their entire life and finding these children suddenly terrified of the parent for no reason that the parent caused? These children are in fact so terrified that they cannot stand to be in the same room with the parent, so they try to hide. If you could take that hurt and multiply it many times, you will still not come close to the hurt that God felt at the rejection of His presence by His beloved humanity.

In verse 9 God meets humanity at their fallen level and interacts with humanity in a way that will benefit it most. God knew that Adam and Eve are now alienated from each other and Himself. God must call out to His humanity because His humanity will no longer call out to Him. God calls out to Adam because Adam had the responsibility for the protection of the Garden and everything in the Garden—including Eve.

Verse 9 also shows something of the anguish God felt when He cries out to His beloved humanity and asks, "Where are you?" God being God knew where they were physically, but He cannot find the relationship or feel the communion anymore. His beloved humanity is lost to Him. God is also giving humanity the opportunity to say where they are. Everything God says or asked in this situation is not designed to provide God with information; rather, His seeking is designed to provide humanity with opportunity for repair and reconciliation.

God is seeking for that which was lost to Him and giving humanity the opportunity to respond by reaching out to God through telling God where they are. Because Adam is no longer capable of trusting God's love, he misses the opportunity of telling his loving God where he is. Adam instead tells God why he is. Adam tells God in verse 10 of this third chapter of Genesis that he was afraid of Him so that when he heard God, he hid himself because he was naked and ashamed.

All of God's reaction is designed to give humanity opportunity for reconciliation, so He asked the question in verse 11: "Who told you that you were naked? Have you eaten from the tree of which I commanded you that you should not eat?" God is giving another opportunity for Adam to take part in relationship with God. Adam should here confess his breaking of the commandment and ask for forgiveness from his loving God.

Adam no longer trusts his relationship enough to con- fess, so he tries to deflect blame and responsibility to his wife. Adam says in verse 12: "The woman whom you gave to be with me, she gave me of the tree, and I did eat." Herein can be found the scope of the tragedy as Adam's fear and shame cause him to try to make his wife the object of God's punishment as he himself tries to escape it. Adam who declared of his Eve, "This is bone of my bone and flesh of my flesh..." now throws her in harm's way because of his own fear and shame.

Also, Adam became the first human to imply that God was responsible for his failing and the pain caused by hu- man failure when he tells God, "The woman that You gave me...." Adam is implying that God caused him to eat because God gave him this woman. Adam's original nature is warped to the point that his actions no longer resemble his original self. Adam is a completely different being because of the Fall.

God also gives Eve the opportunity to confess in verse 13 when He asked her:" What is this you have done?" Eve, like Adam, no longer has the ability to trust God and rely on God's love for her, so she does not confess what she has done but instead tells God why she has done what she has done. Eve, like Adam, tries to deflect blame and responsibility when she tells God, "The serpent deceived me, and I ate."

God's attempts to illicit a confession and to find some remnant of their original loving relationship that was given to Adam and Eve only. The serpent is not asked a question to give him opportunity to confess because there is not the same level of relationship with the animal, as with His chosen representatives made in His image and likeness and carrying His light.

In verses 14 through 19, God makes three pronouncements that express the destiny of the serpent as well as Eve and Adam.

In verse 14 God begins to pronounce the fallout of the fall of humanity starting with the serpent. God gives a detailed pronouncement of the serpent's judgment, and through the serpent, He is pronouncing judgment on the influence behind the serpent—the fallen angel Lucifer. He tells the serpent, "Because you have done this, you are cursed more than all cattle, And more than any beast of the field; On your belly you shall go, And you shall eat dust All the days of your life."

This pronouncement of the physical change of the serpent is not as important as the pronouncement of the change in Lucifer. This fallen angel, whose name meant "light bearer" would now spend all his remaining days traveling throughout the earth trying to manipulate and destroy fallen humanity. To go on his belly would be to surrender his lofty estate as a fallen light-bearing cherub. Lucifer's destiny would be intertwined with humanity until his power over humanity was broken. Instead of being Lucifer, the fallen light-bearing cherub, he would be the Devil, who attempts to destroy as much of humanity as he can as well as rule the world through that part of humanity that he can manipulate and control. To whatever degree humanity was estranged from God, to that degree the Devil could remove God's protection and influence in humanity.

God's judgment is not His wanting to reach out and destroy humanity; rather, His judgment is always for only
one of two reasons:

1) God chastens us for our own improvement and future good.

2) God reluctantly turns us over to that which we have chosen.

The Devil would manipulate humanity to reject God's light and then accuse humanity before God's declaring that God has no right to intercede on humanity's behalf. The Devil's accusation against humanity has always been that humanity has, as an act of free will, rejected God so He must turn us over to that which our free will has chosen.

Humanity was created out of the dust, and this fallen angel would now figuratively crawl on his belly on the earth, consuming as much dust (humanity) as he could.

God is often blamed for causing what He prophetically announces will happen. God is telling this fallen angel the destiny he has chosen for himself. In verse 15 God goes on to tell this fallen angel about his future by stating, "And I will put enmity between you and the woman, and between your seed and her seed; He shall bruise your head, and you shall bruise his heel."

In this verse God is prophetically telling Lucifer that, for a time, humanity may fall under this fallen angel's in- fluence and he may devour some of humanity during this time, but that God will cause humanity to break the bonds of the Devil's control and become his enemy. On that day that seed or offspring of the woman will bruise or "crush" his head, authority, influence, and Lucifer would bruise the seed of the woman's heel. God is not only prophetically pronouncing the fallen angel's end but is pronouncing that a descendent of the woman will cause that end.

Verse 16 tells God's pronouncement to Eve. Notice that unlike Adam or the serpent, God does not begin speaking to her with the phrase "because you have...." God does not directly connect His pronouncement of Eve's destiny to her actions. Also, unlike Adam and the serpent, God does tell Eve that it is God Who is causing her destiny. God does not tell Adam or the serpent, "I will cause...." Causing enmity between the serpent and the woman is all that God says He caused in the destiny of the serpent. Everything else God just tells the serpent and Adam what will happen because of what they have chosen.

In verse 16 God says to Eve, "I will greatly multiply your sorrow and your conception; in pain you will bring forth children; your desire will be for your husband, and he shall rule over you."

The nature of all physical creation was warped at Eden; therefore, the earth, plants; animals and humanity were destined to change after the Fall. When God gave all of Creation hope by declaring that the offspring of the woman would end the Devil's reign on the earth, God knew this would single her out for attack by the Devil. God caused her increased suffering in conception and childbearing, not by doing anything to her Himself, but by exposing her to increased scrutiny and enmity from the Devil. As the enemy of all souls increased his hold on creation and humanity, he shaped the nature of this world that women would suffer in any way he could create. Her delivery of children became a painful and arduous task because the hatred of the enemy shaped childbirth to be so.

The enmity between the fallen angel and the woman is real and is manifested in the manifold physical, emotional, and mental suffering of women throughout history. In most parts of the world and through most of history, this world has been shaped to facilitate the suffering of woman without much protection—even in the marriage relation- ship. The enemy hates humanity but has a very special hatred for women because he was told by God that his future destruction will come though her.

In verses 17, 18 and 19 God's pronouncements to Adam is the longest and most detailed of the three. Adam was given the original commandment. Adam was responsible to tend and protect the Garden including Eve and everything else in it. Eve was deceived, but Adam willfully disobeyed God to selfishly receive from Eve's hand. The full responsibility of the Fall was Adam's, and throughout all of Scripture and knowledgeable secular history, the Fall of humanity is revealed as "the sin of Adam."

Verses 17, 18 and 19: "Then to Adam he said, because you have heeded the voice of your wife, and have eaten from the tree of which I commanded you, saying, 'You shall not eat of it': cursed is the ground for your sake; in toil you shall eat of it all the days of your life. Both thorns and thistles it shall bring forth for you, and you shall eat the herb of the field. In the sweat of your face you shall eat bread till you return to the ground, for out of it you were taken; for dust you are, and to dust you shall return.

Verse 17 begins with a detailed description of Adam's sin. He selfishly yielded to Eve's voice and willfully transgressed his loving God's commandment that he heard directly from God's own voice. After pronouncing the de- tails of Adam's specific sin, God goes on, just as He did with the serpent, to specifically lay out the destiny that his transgression caused for himself.

God then tells Adam that the ground is now cursed because of him. The nature of the earth has been changed because of his transgression. The authority over the earth that God gave to humanity through Adam now through Adam has been ceded to the fallen angel Lucifer. This fallen angel could shape the world in his image by the manipulation of the will and usurping the authority of fallen humanity.

Instead of expressing God's light and working to sub- due the earth, now Adam's work would consist of scraping out survival from a hostile, unyielding world. The Garden of Eden that Adam would have expanded throughout the earth provided food without toil. Adam's original work was not the scraping out of a living but instead was the ex- pressing and preserving of God's light in the world. Now Adam and his offspring's toil would be directed toward the acquiring of food to eat.

God completes the pronunciation of Adam's chosen destiny by telling him that after spending his days toiling in this hostile world for food that he would not be able to retain his God-given life. After losing the breath of life from God, Adam would die and then disintegrate, becoming again the dust that God first fashioned and into which He breathed life when He originally created Adam.

Within these three pronouncements that God has made can be found the root of and the explanation for much of world history, Biblical truth, and the human condition.

End of scene, end of play, close curtain

Epilogue of Our Play

State of Play

Adam, even in his fallen state, still can exercise a measure of his original powers. Adam exercised this power in verse 20 of third chapter of Genesis when he has the wisdom and foresight to give his wife the name Eve. Eve's name is appropriate to the nature of her role in the future of humanity because Eve literally means "life" or "living." Adam understood that in the future his yet unborn descendants would multiply and fill the earth and thus the significance of Eve as the one from whom all future human life would descend. More importantly God had declared that the seed of the woman would crush the serpent's head. Adam's sin introduced darkness and death by giving the fallen angel the ability to manipulate humanity to humanity's own hurt. However, God had promised victory over the fallen angel, which could be nothing short of the restoration of life, from one of the woman's descendants. Eve was literally the mother of all living humanity, but she would also be figuratively the mother of all humanity restored to God's original life.

In verse 21 God makes tunics of animal skins for Adam and Eve. This God-fashioned covering is significant be- cause Adam and Eve themselves started law-based religion with the wearing of fig leaves. Adam's and Eve's wearing the fig leaf was a weak and inadequate attempt to cover the shame caused by motives, thoughts and actions that were contrary to God's light and to get protection from the darkness expressed by these motives, thoughts and actions. Law-based religion is inadequate to affect the human condition or change the fallen human heart.

Do not misunderstand me. Humanity needs laws and religious dogmas to curb their actions. It is a mistake; how- ever, to believe that adherence to such laws is an indication of goodness or light within man. Man's thoughts and motives are untouched by law and religion. Only man's actions can be curbed, and those not completely because no set of laws or religion can prevent humanity's dark thoughts and motives (in other words, man's dark heart) from bleeding out into his actions in ways ungoverned by law or religious practice. Law and religious dogma also fail to change humanity due to humanity's talent for changing law and religious practice into ways of expressing its dark thoughts and motives.

God hates religion. Religion is humanity's attempt to cover its darkness and justify itself before God and each other. God's plan is not religion but salvation. Salvation is God's specific plan to reconcile lost humanity to Him. Christianity is not a religion but is the organization and ex- pression of God's good news of salvation to His beloved humanity.

God only ever desired relationship with humanity. If law and religious practice are not expressions of thoughts and motives turned toward God, then they fall far short of what God offers and desires. Fallen humanity invented religious practice in Eden in an attempt to cover darkness and the shame it brings. God met humanity on their level by co-opting the human invention of laws and religious dogmas and used this human invention to begin the process of human reconciliation through God's specific plan of salvation.

God created superior, more permanent coverings for Adam and Eve not because God required them to be covered, but because that is what His beloved humanity need- ed and wanted.

The animal skin tunics were also the cause of the first deaths that humanity had to witness. This slaughter could only be another source of horror and shame for Adam and Eve. To witness these deaths and to know that they were caused by their actions would have had to bring

to Adam and Eve, a cold realization of the nature of death as well as a taste of the tragic nature of their new reality.

Necessary Boundary

In verse 22 God says that humanity, only in the mat- ter of understanding good and evil, has become like God himself and is a peer with God. God is expressing the lofty state which humanity had attained—even to its own hurt—being the only creature in Creation to join God in understanding this concept of good and evil. Humanity was created to express the light of God in every motive,

thought and action but fell to become creatures who could only express their own arbitrary notions of what was good and what was evil. Humanity would be manipulated and seduced to increasingly choose evil or darkness by the fallen angel through this arbitrary knowledge of what is good and what is evil. For humanity to live in this fallen state forever—without hope of reprieve—would have been be- yond disaster. In verse 22 God blocked humanity from the tree of life to prevent an eternal fallen state.

May I offer a few words about the tree of life? Much has been mistakenly said about God's putting the tree of the knowledge of good and evil in the Garden and com- manding Adam not to eat from it. I have heard it said that humanity was eventually doomed to fall because it would be impossible to ignore the tree forever. Humanity would have eventually exercised its free will and eaten from the tree at some future time—even if Adam did not eat. This view ignores the choice that Adam always had—a choice of two trees. God never forbade Adam from eating from the tree of life. Adam could have eaten from the tree of life instead of the tree of the knowledge of good and evil at any time.

In Genesis 2:9 Adam had access to the tree of life from the very beginning. In fact, the tree of life is mentioned first and then the tree of the knowledge of good and evil. Not much is told about the tree of life in Scripture, but what is told is revealing. From verse 22 we learn that the fruit of the tree of life has the ability—even after Adam's fall—to give humanity the ability to live forever.

Proverbs 3:18 says that wisdom will be like a tree of life for those who follow it. Note that the verse does not
say that wisdom will be like "the" tree of life but instead says that wisdom will be like "a" tree of life to those who follow it. This distinction says that wisdom is not the tree of life, but the nature of the benefits from wisdom will be similar in nature to at least some of the benefits of the tree of life which was in the Garden of Eden.

Wisdom in Scripture is given by God and is a moral quality—not an intellectual one—and is expressed as good choices, and its benefit is a quality and abundant life. Therefore, one of the benefits of the tree of life is a life of quality and abundance.

Revelations 2:7 reveals that believers who overcome will be given to eat of the tree of life. The fact that this is a future promise for believers and that we are told in Revelations 22:2 that the tree of life will be in the midst of the new heavenly city tells us that the tree of life is an important part of the future reconciliation of humanity to God's original purpose.

This is not the time to further explore the nature of the tree of life at this juncture. It is enough to say here that Adam had a choice from the beginning and was not doomed to fail. In the tree of life Adam could have found a viable life-giving alternative to the tree of the knowledge of good and evil.

The Human Condition, Critical

In verse 23 of Genesis 3 God sends humanity out of the Garden to begin the life of toiling for food. This existence was a far cry from the life of dominion and purpose that Adam and Eve originally enjoyed. Adam and Eve
were created to express the light of God throughout Creation and use their likeness of God to have dominion and subdue the earth. Now Adam and Eve would live only to toil, and through that toil, they would scrape a living from a cursed world that is antagonistic to their very survival. From the time of Adam until now, humanity eats by the sweat of its brow. Our entire world system mimics what we see in the natural world and is toil-based. If we do not toil in the land, then we toil on our jobs, but humanity is under the curse of toil-based survival in this world.

The nature of this meaningless existence has been the subject of much human philosophical, political, and artistic expression. We all recognize this meaninglessness and struggle to find meaning in our lives. We have been hard- wired since Adam to have purpose, and that purpose is to express our individual self as God's light in the material world. The root of much of human suffering is man's failure to be able to do so.

Human history is, for the most part, the story of the corrupting and deforming of humanity's need for purpose and dominion. These corruptions and deformities are lived out as both petty and major as well as both individual and corporate atrocities against one another and the world. The scope of the Fall of humanity and the subsequent ex- pulsion from Eden is the single-most important fact that explains the human condition.

In verse 24 God sets cherubim with flaming swords to ensure that humanity cannot return to the tree of life and bring eternal

darkness onto itself. It should give man the utmost joy to remember that in Revelation 2:7 the living God has made provision for humanity to have another
shot at choosing the tree of life.

Everything in the Bible that comes after the first three chapters of Genesis (and everything in history for that matter) is the history of God's specific plan to reconcile fallen humanity to Him. Human beings are the only creations in the universe that can say "No" to God. God's toil is the working of His plan amongst this fallen humanity that is constantly deceived into rejecting His love; God's love is ever working to again allow humanity access to the tree of life.

End Scene, End Epilogue, Close Curtain

Chapter 3 The Fallout

The New Normal

The events contained in the first three chapters of Genesis have ramifications that ripple throughout the rest of the Bible and human history. Nothing is contained in the Bible or human history from Genesis chapter 4 forward that is not an unfolding of those first three chapters. The nature of everything created became warped and twisted away from its original state.

Genesis 1:30 says that the animals in the Garden were given every green herb for food. After the Fall, some green herbs are not only of no nutritional value, now some are actually poisoned.

This generic term for life God uses regarding the animals is not the spiritual life that He breathed into humanity; rather, it is physical life. All animals in the Garden sustained their life as plant eaters. Very shortly after the Fall, Scripture reveals that animals became violent, and many of them sustain their life through the killing and consuming of other animals. The violent nature of the animal kingdom after the Fall was vastly different from what God created in Eden.

The nature of the animal kingdom is just a small part of the warping of Creation. War, famine, and natural disaster would not exist in an Edenic-expanded world. Because of the Fall, the destiny of the earth was altered to reflect a sick, twisted version of God's original creation. Many things accepted as normal in our world every day is in direct opposition to the will and original purposes of God.

The Unfolding of the Two Religions

In Genesis 4:1-8 can be found the unfolding of religious dogma. Cain and his brother Abel are worshipping God with the first fruits of their toil. Nothing can be found in Scripture that would lead us to believe that God request- ed this sacrificing of the first fruits by the brothers. Their religious sacrifice—like the fig leaf before it—is what humanity used to cover the shame and alienation from God due to the Fall. God accepted the sacrifice of the brothers because the committing of the first fruits of their toil to- ward God could be an avenue for humanity to turn a portion of their thoughts and motives toward God and once again feel some semblance of relationship with Him.

However, Cain's sacrifice was not accepted by God when Abel's sacrifice was accepted. The only value any religious practice has is to turn the thoughts and motives of the practitioner toward the light of God. If any religious practice falls short of that goal, it has no value to God or the practitioner. No religious practice has the ability to change humanity's fallen nature; only salvation can do that. No matter what religion is practiced, man's thoughts, motives and actions have been corrupted by the Fall.

Cain's sacrifice was not accepted by God because his religion was an attempt to cover his shame and guilt as a result of his fallen thoughts and motives. Cain's sacrifice was a fig leaf—an attempt to cover his fallen nature and appear righteous before God and humanity. Abel's sacrifice was the result of his thoughts and motives turned toward seeking to cultivate a relationship with God.

Even in our current day, religious practice can look as identical as Cain's and Abel's but actually be polar opposites. Cain's religion is pride-based and concerned with appearing righteous before God and humanity. Abel's religion is relationship-based and seeks relationship with God. Cain's religion is based on the following of religious practice so that his actions will be good enough to be accepted by God and approved by others. Abel's religion is only concerned with a relationship with God, and his actions are an expression of his thoughts and motives while passionately seeking the light of God. Only two religions have existed in the world: the vertical religion of Abel and the horizontal religion of Cain.

Verses 6 and 7 of the fourth chapter of Genesis reveal that Cain's reaction to God's not accepting his sacrifice is anger. God seeks out Cain and tries to reason with him. God tells Cain that if he will do well, his sacrifice will also be accepted. God also warns Cain that if he will not do well, sin lies at his door and seeks to master him but that he can master it.

God is giving Cain an opportunity to respond to Him because God is only concerned with relationship with us. God is not concerned with sacrifice or the keeping of rules and religious dogmas. God knows that if we enter into relationship with Him, then that relationship will fill our thoughts and motives and be expressed in our actions without the need for exterior rules and dogmas. These exterior rules and dogmas applied from the outside to re- strain our actions are the enemy of a relationship with God that is expressed from the inside as a Godly lifestyle.

Cain's anger is the best evidence that his thoughts and motives are not turned toward seeking God. Cain's choosing to direct his anger toward his brother is not rational or logical. His brother Abel had nothing to do with God's rejecting Cain's sacrifice nor could Abel affect God's acceptance of Cain's sacrifice in any way.

What can be seen is a chilling unfolding of Adam and Eve's fig leaf religion into the selfish, prideful religion of Cain. Cain's covering of his sinful thoughts and motives were rejected by God, and instead of turning toward God, he turns further away in anger and jealousy.

In Genesis 4:8, Cain kills his brother Abel. The only rea- son Cain would kill his brother is because Abel's sacrifice was accepted when Cain's was not. Throughout the Bible and secular history, the horizontal religion of Cain can be seen persecuting the vertical religion of Abel. It should not be a surprise then that Israel persecuted and killed many of their own prophets and even hated and plotted to kill Je- sus. Neither should it be a surprise that Christians regularly killed other Christians. The Spanish Inquisition is probably the worst example of the religion of Cain being expressed in the world. The religion of Cain is not limited to Jewish and Christian expression. Whenever religiously based violence, hatred and persecution can be found, the evolution of the religion of Cain in this modern world can be witnessed. When individuals or groups express in patience
and in love the truth of the Bible, the religion of Abel is being encountered.

The story of Cain and Abel is but one example of the unfolding of darkness that was unleashed in Eden with humanity's Fall. The enemy of God and all humanity is pressing his advantage along tens of thousands of different battle fronts to express in the world through human authority the darkness of his will. This is the fallout from the Fall of humanity.

The Battle Lines and the Question of Evil

"The greatest trick the Devil ever played was convincing the world he did not exist."

–Charles Baudelaire

The name Satan means "accuser." Satan must accuse humanity before God. These accusations are a key to his usurping of human authority. As I have already stated, human beings are the only creation in the universe that can say "No" to God, and when humanity says "No," God must eventually turn humanity over to what it has chosen. God will, even in this turning over, seek to protect humanity and to reach out to it. As soon as any individual or group of humans says "Yes" to God, it always remains His good pleasure to intercede for them. The bottom line is human will and human choice remains unchecked by God, and every person chooses or rejects a relationship with God.

The battle between God and the enemy is not the battle between two equals. This battle is between an all-powerful loving God versus a deceiver and a slanderer of humanity competing for the hearts of people in the midst of humanity's fallen state and free will.

If the enemy can manipulate humanity into rejecting God and then successfully accuse humanity of rejecting God, then God would have to turn man over to what he has chosen—namely the will of the enemy. God would have no grounds to intercede on humanity's behalf be- cause humanity's free will would have chosen other than God.

In the book of Job, the veil of the curtain is pulled back to give a rare and firsthand glimpse of this struggle. The first five verses of the first chapter of Job tell of Job's righteousness. No fallen human being is perfect, but Job's thoughts and motives are obviously turned toward God and expressed in his actions. Job is carefully living a life that acknowledges God first, and he is living this life for himself and his family. Job's heart is pointed constantly toward God; his is the vertical religion of Abel. Job's astute life before God, however, does not guarantee a life free from worldly trouble.

In the sixth verse, the enemy presents himself before God. The term sons of God can refer to angels, but Adam was also referred to as "the son of God." Luke 3:38 Adam, as a created son of God, would speak with God in person in the Garden in the cool of the evening. The enemy, now with the sons of God (the angels) presents himself before God.

If it were not for the Fall, humanity would be able to have direct access and commune directly with God as the one who represents God on the earth. Instead of humanity, the enemy presents himself before God and speaks of
his role on the earth.

In Job1:7 God asked the enemy from where he has come. This is not a question of curiosity because God knows all, but God is establishing the limits of the enemy's influence in the earth. Where the enemy is welcome and where he is permitted on the earth tells of his influence and authority in the earth.

The enemy begins to brag of his influence and access; this bragging is also an accusation against humanity. The enemy is saying, "I have gone and can continue to go throughout the world because humanity has rejected You and accepted me."

God in verse 8 then corrects the enemy by saying, "Your influence is not over everyone. My servant Job's thoughts and motives our turned toward me."

In verses 9 through 10 the enemy specifically accuses Job by telling God that Job's thoughts and motives are not turned toward God but toward himself. He intimates that Job serves God because God protects his possessions— not because he wants relationship with God. The enemy then tells God that if God would take all that Job has, Job would no longer serve Him.

The only thing restraining the enemy from completely overwhelming humanity with world devastation and suffering was the intercession of God in human history. God's intercession was dependent on God's having human representation in the earth. An individual or a group, who as an act of their free will chose God, would be choosing God's governance and intercession in their lives and through their lives God's governance and intercession to the world. God must answer this accusation of the enemy. If there is truly no one in the earth whose free will is turned to God and every person serves the enemy, then God will not override human free will as expressed as the complete corporate human rejection of God in the affairs of humanity. God removes the hedge of His protection from around Job in verse 12, and immediately the scope of the enemy's usurped authority over man and Creation can be seen in verses 13 through 19. With two acts of controlling human beings—one act of controlling nature (namely the wind) and one act of the supernatural (namely fire or lighting falling from the sky), Satan rapidly devastates all of Job's possessions, including his children. In the case of the fire's falling from the sky, see how quickly what the enemy has done is attributed to God. The lone survivor of the fire from the sky tells Job in verse 16 that the "...fire of God fell from heaven."

Much too often our natural disasters, wicked acts of humanity, or unexplainable calamities are blamed on God. The words, "act of God", are often used when the words act of the enemy should be employed.

Job's reaction in verse 20 and 21 shows that his relationship with God is not based on his possessions. He acknowledges that he came in the world with nothing and all that he had was given by God; therefore, God could take it if He wanted. Job blesses God's name.

In Job 2:1 through 6, a repeat episode of Satan's bragging takes place, and God responds that Job is not under Satan's sway even though he devastated his possessions. This time the enemy's accusation involved Job's health. Again, God must answer this accusation, so He allows the enemy to affect Job's body but sets a boundary protecting Job's life. Here the enemy is displaying his usurped authority over human health.

We often ask why God would afflict disease and suffering on the world but when the curtain is pulled back, we see it is the enemy behind the world's disease and suffering. God is constantly moving on Humanity's behalf, searching for individuals and groups that he can use as a conduit to pour protection and blessing into the chaos of fallen human history.

In verse 7 the enemy afflicts Jobs body. Job's wife devastated by her losses, and the sight of her husband's suffering, attributes all his suffering to God. She tells Job to curse God and die to end his suffering. Job will yet not break relationship with God. Job in his reply to his wife also does not acknowledge the role of the enemy in his suffering. Job does not break fellowship with God, but he assumes his plight is from God. Job attributes all that has happened to him to the arbitrary choices of God.

How often have any of us felt like Job? How often have we been disappointed or even angry with God for events in our lives, or in the world around us, that seem arbitrary or unexplainable? What would we see if we could look behind the veil and witness the heavenly struggle going on just above world events? Although his plight is caused by Satan Job is right in the sense that God has allowed it. Yes, it is God behind his suffering but more accurately it is God maintaining Job as a representative in the earth and as a conduit for Godly blessing and intercession in human affairs.

Job, of course, does not know this. He will not give up his relationship with God, but he does question why God would do this to him. Job knows he is not perfect but cannot understand why this has happen to him when he is doing everything in his power to serve God. He spends the main portion of the book of Job answering his three friends who somehow try to blame Job for what God has allowed.

Job has many questions he would ask God. Job states some of these questions while he is being accused by his friends. Job's questions may sound familiar to us because we have asked similar questions ourselves. Why do good people suffer? Why is there so much evil in the world and why do so many evil people seem to prosper? God, I pray and do everything you ask but it seems like you do not hear me or worse you do not care.

God's answers Job in the 38th chapter of the book He never explains what has been going on behind the veil. Job will never know his role in the rebuking of satanic authority or the righteousness with which God esteemed him. These things are not what is best for Job's life. For God, the most important thing is to improve His relationship with his servant Job by giving him a deeper understanding of who He is.

In that 38th chapter God answer Job out of the whirlwind with questions of his own; "Who is this that darkens counsel with words without knowledge? Dress for action like a man; I will question you, and you make known to me. Where were you when I laid the foundation of the earth? Tell me if you have understanding. Who determined its measurements - surely you know!"

God goes on to ask Job question after question. Each question asked by God out of the whirlwind makes Job more and more aware that his human understanding is inadequate to begin to comprehend the majesty and the wisdom behind the workings ofGod in the earth. God is God and we are rarely able to look behind the veil and even if God allowed this, we could not fathom what we saw.

Job is humbled and in chapter 42 beginning at verse 2 he replied, "I know that you can do all things, and no purpose of yours can be thwarted." He goes on to acknowledge that it was foolish of him to question God. He has had a glimpse of Gods majesty in the whirlwind and a glimpse of God's wisdom from God's questions. Even though Job still does not understand why all this has happened to him he has learned that all such questions and accusations against God are foolish.

Yes, there is much that happens to us specifically and in the world in general that defies explanation in light of the existence of a loving God. There is nothing that can be said to someone who has suffered or witnessed suffering in the world justify it. There are two facts however that our undeniable in this world.

1) There is a malevolent entity that is constantly working to usurp Humanity's original powers and authorities for the purposes of destroying as many humans as it can.

2) There are battles and strategies instituted by God on our behalf that we will never know about and even if we could peek behind the veil, we could not begin to comprehend them.

We must acknowledge that God's ways are so beyond our understanding and what happens behind the veil is so far above our comprehension that, like Job, we have to believe that the only viable approach to God is one of faith.

God's Plan

The seed of the woman

God's promise of the seed of the woman wounding the serpent's head is the only flicker of hope in the pronouncement of the fallen destiny of humanity. This flicker of hope was fanned into flame in the land of Judah in the district of Galilee and the city of Nazareth. Jesus from Nazareth was this promised seed of the woman.

In the Gospel of Luke in the 1st chapter beginning at the 26th verse we are told how God gave to fallen humanity the one who would deliver us from the power of the enemy. In verse 26 God sends the angel Gabriel to a virgin girl in Nazareth to announce that she would conceive in her womb a son who will be called Jesus. Jesus is Greek for the Hebrew name Joshua and Joshua means "Jehovah the savior" or "God is our salvation." God's promise of saving his lost Humanity was being fulfilled in the birth of Jesus.

There has been much debate as to whether Jesus was really the product of a virgin berth. This question can only be asked by people who are unfamiliar with the first three chapters of Genesis.

Humanity, because of the fall, could only procreate other fallen human beings in its image and likeness. For someone to not be in the image and likeness of fallen humanity that being could not be conceived by a fallen man and woman. Furthermore, if God spoke creation into existence, formed Adam out of the dust and fashioned Eve from a rib taken from Adam it would be a small thing for God to fashion conception in a virgin's womb. Although fashion by God Jesus was born like any other human baby. Luke 2:6-7

Jesus, because he was conceived in Mary's womb and grew in her womb like any other human, was as human as anyone else born of a woman. Jesus, because he was formed in the womb by the spirit of God was also the son of God and did not inherit Adam's fallen condition. For the first time in history someone was born of a woman who was not part of fallen humanity yet could walk in the original authority of Adam. The prophecy of the seed of the woman had been fulfilled.

We read throughout the Gospels how Jesus exercised his authority as the son of man. A human born that fully inherited the authority God intended when he created humanity. Jesus exercised his authority over physical disease, spiritual oppression, and nature. Jesus exercised this authority to demonstrate that the son of man had authority over the works of the Devil.

The son of God

In the Gospel of John beginning at the first chapter and first verse we are told what it meant for Jesus to be the son of God. The Word was God and the Word was with God. Through the Word everything was made, and the Word became flesh and lived among humanity. Jesus is the son of God but we are told in the New Testament book of Philippians in the 2nd chapter and the 6th through the 8th verse that Jesus set aside his deity, his God nature, to live as the son of man. This was crucial for humanity. In order to occupy Humanity's rightful place in Creation Jesus had to live completely as a human. What we see in Jesus is a human being exercising the full authority given to humanity in Eden. Even though Jesus was God in the flesh (God expressed through a soul and body), and the eternal Word made known, he exercised none of that nature.

This is a great mystery. God was made flesh but humbled himself and lived as a human being.

The last Adam

In the book of 1st Corinthians the15th chapter and 45th verse we read "The first man Adam became a living being, but the last Adam became a life-giving spirit." In Genesis we learned how the first Adam became a living being. In the Gospels we learn how Jesus, the last Adam, became a life-giving spirit. Jesus took the place of the first Adam as the progenitor of humanity. The first Adam was the progenitor of every fallen human being. The last Adam, Jesus, was the progenitor of every human made spiritually alive.

As a sinless Adam Jesus was not part of Humanity's fallen nature and death. He was the only human that Satan could not accuse, and he was the only one that did not inherit death. Jesus, the last Adam, could live in obedience to God. Were the first Adam failed in obedience the last Adam could succeed.

As the obedient last Adam Jesus did not have the pronouncement of death on his destiny. Jesus however could choose to take on this pronouncement in place of fallen humanity. Jesus could take on Humanity's death so that humanity could again have eternal life. Jesus could take on himself the death sentence that the first Adam earned for humanity and as the last Adam, through his obedience, earn a spiritual life sentence for all of humanity. All humanity that was spirituality born through him could escape the original Adam's death. We are told in the New Testament book of 1st Corinthians in the 22nd verse that in Adam all died in Jesus all are made alive.

Through the last Adam humanity can once again take its rightful place and exercise dominion over the earth and take authority over the works of the Devil. This authority expresses itself as expressing God's light in creation through freeing other humans from the Devils influence and introduces them to this new eternal life granted humanity by this second Adam.

But just as Cain slew righteous Abel the part of humanity who is not submitted to God is manipulated by the enemy to stand in opposition to anything or anyone that represents God. The war that is currently waging is God through the followers of Jesus is rescuing as many humans as possible from the enemy and the enemy trying to destroy as much of humanity as possible through human manipulation. The irony of this war is that because Christians fight against an unseen enemy and not against other human beings the majority of humanity is not aware that this war is even being fought or what is at stake.

Hell

The good news that Jesus preached was that anyone who was willing could escape hell and receive from him eternal life. It was of the utmost importance to him, more important than physical healing, battling poverty or following religious tradition. Hell is a real place and Jesus described it as such.

What hell is not however is a place that God created to send bad people for sinning. In Matthew, the 25th chapter the 41st verse we read that hell was prepared for the Devil and his angels. It is true that human beings will end up there, but only because they have remained part of the Devil's rebellion that all humanity became a part of through the deception and fall in Eden.

God prepared hell for the Devil and his angel's but prepared provision, mercy, love, and a free way to return to him for humanity. The central desire of the enemy is to deceive as many people as possible and cause them to reject the love of God and the good news of redemption. He wants to carry as much of humanity into his eternal torment and separation from God as possible.

The entire effort of God displayed in scripture and human history is the passionate continued rescue of humanity from hell. We have talked about the evil and suffering in our world and our frustration with God because of it. Know this; the alleviation of human suffering in this world is a secondary consideration to God compared to the rescuing of humanity from hell. Whenever someone goes to hell it is to God like one of his children has been kidnapped and carried away to a place of torment forever.

God's own messengers have been murdered and tortured from the murder of Abel to the martyrs of this present day to secure eternal life for humanity. The sacrifices of these believers have been made in order to fulfill the primary mission of God. This mission is the rescue of as many people as possible from sharing in a judgment that was not created for them but for the enemy and his fallen angels.

Before the foundation of the world

One might ask but what about all the people who were born and died before Jesus took on their sin. In the book of Revelation, the 13th chapter the 8th verse we are told that the lamb was slain before the foundation of the world. There is a lot of symbolism in and around this scripture but the only thing we need to understand for our purposes is that "the lamb slain" is symbolism for Jesus. This scripture tells us that the lamb (Jesus) was slain before the world was created. How is this possible? The biblical text and Secular roman history tell us that Jesus was Crucified about 30 A. D. The answer to this mystery is time vs. eternity.

Time is a liner progression, but eternity is the infinite present. Spiritual events, like the crucifixion of Jesus, happen at a fixed point in the progression of time but the same spiritual event exists throughout all of eternity. The nature of eternity is that events cannot have a fixed point. If something exists or is true in eternity it has always and will always exist in eternity. Therefore, it was important for humanity not to eat from the tree of life and take our fallen state into eternity where it would have eternal existence.

In the context of time no human could benefit from the last Adam giving humanity a new spiritual birth before approximately 30 A.D. In the context of eternity every human that entered eternity through death could benefit from the spiritual birth of Jesus.

One may also ask by what standard are those who had no chance to accept Christ, because they lived and died before Christ entered the world, to be accepted into spiritual rebirth? In the book of Romans, the 2nd chapter the 19th and 20th verses tell us that from the beginning of the world God has been revealed to humanity by God himself. God's invisible attributes are easily seen. This is a paradox; invisible attributes, easily seen? God's invisible attributes are revealed to humanity through revelation by faith.

In Romans, the 2nd chapter 16th and17th verse we are told that the righteousness of God is revealed in the Gospel (Good news of Jesus) from faith to faith. In Romans, the 4th chapter the 9th verse we are also told that Abraham's faith was credited to him as righteousness. Throughout history even before the Jewish law if someone had faith in God it was counted by God as righteousness. Remember Job. Job never claimed perfection, but he had faith in God, and we know from that story God called Job righteous. From the beginning of the world if someone's thoughts and motives were turned to God that person was credited by God with righteousness.

Remember Cain and Abel. God accepted Abel's sacrifice because his thoughts and motives, or his faith, was turned to God. God accepted the faith of people before they had any knowledge of Jesus. When humans responded to God to the utmost of their ability and knowledge God honors that and credits them with righteousness.

In "time" humanity before the sacrifice of Jesus could not enjoy its full benefits but when Abel, Abraham, David etc. entered eternity salvation becomes theirs because of their life of faith.

What Jesus means to the world

We have read in Job how Satan stood in Adam's place in heaven by means of his usurped authority over the earth. We also read how he accused humanity so that God would have no grounds to intercede on Humanity's behalf.

In Revelation the 12th chapter we find the story of Jesus and the breaking of Satanic authority. The book of revelation is full of symbolism and mysteries. It tells us the complete history of the great spiritual struggle from the beginning to the end. For our purposes we will focus only on the symbolism in these scriptures pertaining to the birth of Christ and the displacement of the Devil.

In verse 1 and 2 of chapter 12 of the book of revelation, we are given the symbolism of a woman with a garland of twelve stars. This woman is Israel and the garland of 12 stars represents the 12 tribes and the twelve patriarchs of Israel. This woman is with child and in great pain to give birth. The great pain of the woman giving birth is the pain caused by the enemy. The enemy knew that the promised seed of the woman would come through Israel, so he tried to destroy Israel again and again. He persecuted Israel at every opportunity. At the time of the birth of Jesus Israel was being oppressed by Rome. The labor pains are also symbolic of the birth of Jesus being near.

In verse 3 and 4 a great red dragon appears and pulls a third of the stars from the sky and is poised to devour the woman's child. This dragon is the Devil and the third of the stars is a third of the heavenly angels that joined his rebellion. The Devil knowing that the birth of the Christ is near puts every human influence at his disposal to destroy the child. The killing of all the children two years old and younger by Herod was a part of the Devil's attempt to devour Jesus. Herod's murder of the innocent children is found in The Gospel of Matthew the 2nd chapter 13th verse.

In verse 5 and 6 of this 12th chapter of Revelation Israel gives birth to Jesus. Jesus lives his life and triumphs over the Devil and is taken up to heaven to his thrown. In verse 7 and 8 war broke out in heaven. Now that Jesus won victory over the power of the Devil, and through that victory, man again had access to God, the Devil no longer had a rightful place to stand in heaven through Man's usurped authority. The Devil was cast down from heaven and his angels with him. Verse 9 tells us that the Devil is that ancient serpent; he expressed himself through the serpent in Eden, who has deceived the whole world. The whole world is under the Devil's influence. Verse 10 tells us that salvation and the power of Christ has come, and the accuser of the brethren was cast down. We witnessed this accusing firsthand behind the veil in the book of Job.

ll of this that we read in these verses is a result of the victory of the death and resurrection of Jesus. Through this victory humanity again has a choice between the word of God and our own arbitrary knowledge of what is good and evil. Jesus gives the entire world the ability to once again choose life and access to the living God.

The sacrifice of Jesus

The most important mystery in scripture is the one most heard and the one least understood. In the book of John the 3rd chapter and the 16th verse we are told that God loved humanity so much that he gave his only begotten Son and that anyone who believes in him will not die but will live forever.

We see this scripture on billboards, at sporting events in evangelistic literature. It is one of the most well known and most quoted biblical scriptures in the entire world. How many of us who quote it really comprehend the scope of what is at stake in the acceptance or rejection of those words.

If the first three chapters of Genesis are true then humanity is under a death sentence and God has, from the very beginning, been doing everything he can to call his beloved humanity back to him and away from danger. God's plan for Humanity's rescue is the sacrifice of his only begotten Son (Jesus) to replace his created son (Adam) so that anyone who partakes of his sacrifice can become the adopted children of God and escape death.

Jesus was not killed by the Devil but gave his life in obedience to God his father for our sins. Through his entire earthly ministry Jesus told his followers that he would lay down his life for humanity. This laying down of the life of Christ for our sins is the central mystery of the Christian faith and its acceptance or rejection is life and death to all who hear it.

There is no better illustration of how the mystery of the sacrifice of Jesus for our sins is accepted or rejected than in Luke the 25th chapter the 39th verse through the 43rd verse. When we include the reading of the crucifixion account in the other gospels, we understand that Jesus was crucified with two thieves who at first yelled insults and taunts at him. One of the thieves however came to have a change of heart to the point that he rebuked the other thief who was still taunting and insulting Jesus. Understand there was nothing in material perception that could have convinced the thief that Jesus was a king or was any different than anyone else. In fact, Jesus was bloodied, beaten, crucified, and made fun of with a fake crown of three-inch thorns pressed onto his skull. Yet this thief, who was himself dying on a cross, perceived something in Jesus that made him utter these strange words: "Lord, remember me when you come into your kingdom."

This thief went from taunting Jesus to calling him Lord. This thief also came to believe that Jesus had a kingdom and that he was able to favor him at some future date regarding that kingdom. There was nothing reasonable about this thief's belief. All the evidence of the material world indicated that Jesus was a tortured dying nobody and could not help himself let alone someone else. This is an illustration of revelation at work. This thief responded through faith and received revelation as to who Jesus was. The other thief perceived Jesus through material perception and never knew who he was.

Revelation is totally independent from reason and material perception but is an elevated way of perceiving reality. Revelation is truer to how Adam before the fall perceived his world. It is yet a mystery how two people in identical situations can respond to God's presence in opposite ways. To respond to God with faith and gain understanding through revelation or to reject God through material perception.

These two ways of seeing Jesus are the central, crucial realities of the human condition and the most important decision that will be made by everyone. It is literally a question of eternal life or death.

Conclusion

It is easy to be distracted into turning the question of belief in Jesus into some other question. The question of the belief in Jesus is not a social, political, scientific, psychological, or even a religious question. We tend to pick an issue in one of these categories and decide whether Christianity fits our views on that issue. This is a backward way of examining any belief. We should examine Christianity on its own merits and separate from any other issue. Is a faith in Jesus sustainable and credible, and will I through faith adhere to this belief, is the only issue that is relevant. When you decide the question of Jesus on its own merit then you can let that choice inform your stance on the various other issues in your life.

If you should choose to know more about Jesus it is an easy thing to accomplish. Ask the living God, right now were you are, to come into your life and reveal himself to you. Begin to read the Bible for yourself, the gospel of John is a good place to start.

Two things will happen when you do this. You will begin to understand things about God through the Bible that you did not realize before as your faith unlocks revelation. You will also feel opposition in the form of distractions and doubt. The good news is; if you want to know God through Jesus there is no power in the universe that can prevent God from revealing himself to you.

What say you of Jesus?

180

Be the Message!